# TORN INSIDE OUT:
## Releasing Grief 40 Years Later

## By Jo Ann Wentland Koch

TORN INSIDE OUT: Releasing Grief 40 Years Later

Cover photographs courtesy of The Carter Studio, Berlin, WI 1955
Cover design by Velicer Design, Green Bay, WI
All photos and scans in this book belong to the author, Jo Ann Wentland Koch. None may be copied without the author's written permission.

Your Publishing Source LLC
www.YourPublishingSource.com

## DEDICATION

I dedicate this book to my departed family who experienced an
unimaginable misfortune. A family who did their best in
coping with losses and shattered dreams.

# Contents

# ACKNOWLEDGEMENTS

For over forty years I attempted to suppress memories of the events that occurred in1955. Once I began writing, thoughts and recollections from others, who also were affected, became necessary and helpful.

My sincere thanks and gratitude go to the following people for making it possible for me to write this book:

- My extended family of cousins who were gracious and willing to recall events of the year 1955.

- My cousin Steve Webber who has been our family historian for many years.

- My friends and friends of my brother John who recalled helpful events from the past.

- My husband Butch who was always helpful, supportive, patient, and encouraging to me in this endeavor.

- Our daughters, Kim and Kristin, for their interest, questions, and support in learning about their family.

- To Barbara Gusick, Ron La Point, and Jo Zorr - readers of my manuscript - for their generous sharing of time, suggestions, and advice.

- Carolyn Dargevics who was patient and instrumental in editing, organizing, and arranging my writings for publication.

# FOREWORD

By Butch Koch

A person is influenced by events that shape their actions, emotions, and life. Jo, my wife, is someone who has taken the lemons that she received in her early life and made them into lemonade. While adversity can either weaken or strengthen a person, she has gained resilience in managing her trauma.

Jo is a very loving, compassionate, caring, and prayerful person. She has the personality and ability to meet strangers, listen to their problems, and five minutes later, know some deep aspect of their life and, if need be, will add that person to her prayer list. Her first thoughts are not for herself but for others. She is the most thoughtful person I know. Jo has spent thousands of hours volunteering with various civic and church groups that help others. She has logged over 2000 hours with one group that screens children.

Back in the 1950s, therapy was not offered to the Wentland family. People and families usually would cope with tragedy by just not talking about it. Years later, Jo found that, though emotionally difficult, writing about her family had the cathartic effect she needed. This book is the result of years spent writing her thoughts about the events in her life.

One effect of the polio ordeal on her life is that three years after the tragedy in her family, Jo was diagnosed with Type I Diabetes. I, along with many in the medical field, believe this came as a result of the virus,

ix

the shock, and the stress that these events caused. Throughout the 53 years of dealing with this disease, she has worked with dedication and determination to control and prevent the devastation that diabetes can cause. This has been a worthwhile effort, allowing her to have an active and normal life. There have been problems and setbacks, as in 1990 she received a surgery for seven heart bypasses. However, during our 48 years of marriage, I have never heard her complain of the inconvenience, work, and fear that her health problems have caused.

A person is not defined by the adversity they face; rather, they are defined by how they *respond* to that adversity. I believe that the positive effects her ordeals have had on her life have made her into the strong, loving, and caring role model that she is. Jo is a beautiful person inside and outside; she is the love of my life and MY HERO.

Jo and Butch – 2010

# INTRODUCTION

"If you cry, you are selfish," words exclaimed through my mother's tense lips shortly after the tragic death of my sister and brother. Those penetrating words, spoken with her finger pointing directly in the face of a 12-year-old girl, are vivid memories of some 57 years.

My mother was a caring and loving woman who, at the age of 41, lost two of her four children. Her life was filled with misfortune that began when she was a child in the 1920s. Unfortunately, at that time and when her children died, silence was how people dealt with tragedy. Coping was your personal, private dilemma. "Men don't cry" was customary; I never witnessed my father or my older brother crying. My cousins, aunts and uncles, grandparents, friends, and even our family minister didn't know what to do or say; so they remained silent. I cried. My mother cried. Our sorrow was so visibly wrenching that my mother decided we couldn't continue living in this manner; so she issued that order to me, and I obeyed. I immediately held my tears and emotions so I wouldn't be "selfish."

For years, I silently, in my heart, suffered and painfully mourned the loss of my siblings – many thoughts every day. Missing them and thinking of the way they died was a big part of every day. I couldn't avoid thinking of them. I held these feelings locked inside until I attended a life story writing class more than 40 years after their deaths. So I began to write.

My writings focused on my family and our horrible experiences. It helped me to unlock the feelings in my heart that had been imprisoned for so long. I was finally able to cry the tears I had blinked back all those years. I felt I was being torn inside out. Writing has helped me in the healing process but has not answered the question of why I was the only child in my family to be spared the effects of polio.

I gained compassion for families who have lost their children. After August 1955, at age 12, I began to say a short prayer each time I read or heard of the death of a child. My prayer, "God, please be with the grieving family."

The months June, July, and August left an indelible, heartbreaking impression in my life. The twins, my older siblings, celebrated their 14th birthdays on June 13, 1955. Jeanie died on August 21; Georgie on August 27. These two months between their birthdays and their deaths became untouchable dates for me. I planned May 24 as our wedding day. Our two children were born in September and December. I avoided activities in those three months whenever possible, and unlike other people, I would be happy summer was over.

# A TRAGIC AUGUST

*Jo Ann Wentland Koch*

## SIX DAYS THAT CHANGED OUR LIVES FOREVER

August 1955 began with an eager anticipation but would end in unbearable tragedy. In a month, my older brother, Jack, who was 15 years old, would be starting his junior year in high school. The twins, Georgie and Jeanie, had celebrated their 14th birthdays in June and were anxious to begin their freshman year. I was 12 and starting eighth grade. Both twins had saved money in anticipation of shopping for needed clothes and school items.

My brother, Georgie, mowed lawns for several people in the town after buying a big, old power mower at a yard sale. He was very proud of his purchase and loved the noise it made as he propelled it down the middle of the street as he traveled from job to job. He bought the gas it needed, and we laughed about the money it cost him just to get to his jobs. He also earned money with an afternoon paper route. He saved his money, but he always bought a treat for his friend Jeffrey or me when we helped him deliver newspapers.

My sister Jeanie and I were given an allowance for the weekly cleaning of our house and doing the family laundry. Her shopping list included two bras, undies, socks, blouse, and a skirt. Our plan was to shop in Madison the week before school started. That summer, she had taught herself to sew using our mother's pedal sewing machine. I was mesmerized by her ability to simultaneously pedal the machine with her feet and push the material along with her hands. She sewed a pink and white flowered, sleeveless sundress with a full, gathered skirt.

August was exceptionally hot that year. The newspapers and radios reported a polio epidemic moving into areas near and in Wisconsin. My mother was nervous as she and her younger brother George had contracted the disease in the 1920s. My mother did not become as sick as her brother. They did, however, spend months sharing a room in the Madison Sanatorium.

Uncle George suffered with leg paralysis for which he received the Kenny treatment, a method of treating polio, in which hot, moist packs were applied to affected muscles to relieve spasms and pain. A regimen of exercises was prescribed to prevent deformities and to strengthen the muscles. In later years, George was affected with Post- Polio Syndrome, a complication such as muscle weakness affecting the patient 30 to 40 years after the initial polio illness. In the last years of his life, George used a Stair Lift and a Rascal Scooter to aid him in climbing stairs and being mobile.

Because of this experience, my mother knew what might happen to her family. In those early years, polio was known as Infantile Paralysis as children were more often affected than adults.

A circus came to our small town of Berlin in the middle of August, and the show elephants were housed near the train station downtown.

The twins and I hurried to watch the fascinating elephants and their trainers. As we sat on the curb along the street, we enjoyed being near them to witness their training process.

The next day, the three of us attended the circus performance at the fairgrounds on North Wisconsin Street. As we sat under the circus tent, we excitedly watched the performers and animals as they paraded through the open tent doors. We were mesmerized with the loud music and noise as the elephants, we recognized from the day before, performed in front of us.

A few days after the circus performance, Jeanie and I became ill. We suffered from headaches and fevers so our mother treated us with alcohol baths to lower our high temperatures. I recovered; however, Jeanie's high temperature continued.

As she did weekly, my mother wrote a postcard to her stepmother, Grandma Webber, in Madison. Georgie and I read it on the way to the post box on the corner near our house. It stated, "Jeanie isn't feeling well. Georgie is trying to get attention by saying he isn't feeling well." After reading this, Georgie remarked to me, "I'm not making it up. If I die, she will see."

Jeanie insisted my parents not call our doctor because she didn't want to bother him on a Saturday night. She felt so ill that my parents set up a bed downstairs where she could watch television. Jeanie and our family spent the evening watching television which included one of her favorite programs, *The Lawrence Welk Show*.

At 5 a.m. the next morning, Sunday, August 21, I was awakened by the loud noise of a vehicle. I was upstairs in the bedroom Jeanie and I shared. When I looked out the window, I saw an ambulance in our driveway with its loud motor running. I ran downstairs and turned the corner into our living room where I saw Jeanie on a cart with big wheels. She was being moved to the ambulance. I was afraid for her but she smiled at me. Our brother Jack hopped into the ambulance to be with her while my mother followed in our car. The ambulance was taking her to Berlin Memorial Hospital, only one block from our house.

Mrs. Walker, a friend of our family who lived next door to the hospital, recognized my mother near the ambulance entrance and asked what was wrong. My mother motioned for her to stay away and responded, "It isn't good."

A spinal tap was ordered for Jeanie, who had to be positioned on her hands and knees. A needle was placed into her spine to withdraw fluid to be tested. This test diagnosed polio. My dad later told me that Jeanie was bothered with that test, as she was uncovered. Her modesty showed more than her fear of the painful test.

Jeanie was then transferred to the Wisconsin General Hospital in Madison, two hours away. My mother rode in the ambulance with her and noticed Jeanie's fingernails were turning blue before they reached the hospital. Upon arrival, a tracheotomy was performed. This is a surgical operation in which a hole was made into her trachea in the front of her neck to aid in her breathing. Jeanie died 15 minutes after arriving at the hospital.

Meanwhile at home, Georgie and I began to do the weekly laundry. We had a wringer washer and two rinse tubs in our basement. Up the outside steps we would run with a basket of wet laundry to the line. We'd check the clothes on the line and remove the dry ones to make more room for the next batch of wet laundry.

By 11:00 a.m., the washing was done. I went outside to remove and fold what was dry, and as I entered our backdoor with a big basket of folded laundry, I saw a large man standing in our living room. Dr. Wiesender, the City Health Officer, was talking to my father who was sitting on the sofa. The doctor's abrupt words spoken to my father were "Jeanie is dead."

As I put the laundry on the table, my father looked up at me and said, "We lost Jeanie." I asked what he meant. I pictured an ambulance that had run off the road and was lost in a wooded area. They could certainly find it, I thought. Then he said, "She didn't make it." I then asked if that meant she died, and he nodded.

I ran outside to tell Georgie who was lying in a hammock. He bolted upright and said he didn't believe me. As he ran into the house, I ran to the gas station next door. I did not want to return home as I felt my father would certainly die of a heart attack or return to drinking. Gene, the attendant and close friend of our older brother Jack, assured me my dad would be okay.

At 11:30 that morning, we were told Jeanie had polio, and had died shortly after arriving at the hospital. We were told later that it was the type of polio called bulbar, the kind that paralyzes the muscles to the lungs. Georgie couldn't believe his twin sister had died, and he kept repeating, "My twin, my twin."

The moment my father's boss, Rolly, heard of Jeanie's death, he arrived at our front door and offered his help. I asked Rolly if my father could have that afternoon off work.

Later that afternoon my father went to the meat market for our supper. By habit, he ordered six pork chops. When he returned home - and with a tear in his eye, he told me about the oversight of ordering more meat than needed.

# Berlin Girl, 14, Dies Of Polio; Situation Not As Bad As Rumors Have It

## Five Cases In Berlin Area, 2 New Cases

Jeannette Alice Wentland, 14, daughter of Mr. and Mrs. Harvey Wentland, 109 Spring St., Berlin, died at Wisconsin General Hospital, Madison, Sunday morning, of polio.

She had complained of feeling ill Saturday evening and was taken to Berlin Memorial Hospital at 6 a.m. Sunday in an extremely weak condition. After examination by a local physician she was rushed to Madison, where she died 15 minutes after arriving at the hospital.

One other new case, Jon McConnell, 25, of Berlin, was reported by Dr. A. J. Wiesender, city health officer, this week. McConnell was sent to Wausau Hospital Saturday, but his case was not believed to be serious.

**THE TWO NEW** cases brought the total of polio cases to five in the Berlin area. Of the five, the Wentland girl died, and two have returned home from the isolation ward at Wausau Hospital. Ralph O'Kon and Dennis Schroeder are both on the road to recovery. Robin Sanders of Berlin remained at Berlin Memorial Hospital.

Mrs. Walter Losinski of Princeton, county chairman of the National Foundation for Infantile Paralysis, said no cases had been reported in the county other than those in the Berlin area. She said there was one case rumored in Dalton, but she had received no confirmation.

Mrs. Losinski said she had been informed by Dr. Alfred T. Lieninger, health officer of the village of Green Lake, that three rumored cases in that village had been definitely established as rumors.

**THE RUMOR MILL** was buzzing in Berlin early this week, too. There were reports of as many as a dozen cases in Berlin alone, and almost everyone who went to the doctor — and certainly anyone admitted to the hospital — was immediately believed to have polio, as far as the rumor mill was concerned.

One case widely reported as "definitely" polio turned out to be ptomaine poisoning, and the patient was released after two days in the hospital. A local chiropractor said he had a half dozen persons in his office Monday who had pains in their limbs, and who were sure they had polio. But the usual treatment brought comfort, he said.

# Polio Claims Life Of Berlin School Girl

BERLIN — Polio stuck out its ugly hand here this weekend to take the life of a 14-year-old girl and send another from here to the isolation hospital in Wausau.

Jeannette Alice Wentland, 14, daughter of Mr. and Mrs. Harvey Wentland of 109 Spring St., died Sunday morning in Wisconsin General Hospital, Madison, after being taken from the hospital here earlier in the morning. She had complained of feeling ill Saturday evening, and was taken to Berlin Memorial Hospital about 6 a.m. Sunday in a very weak condition. After diagnosis there by Dr. H. C. Koch, the girl was immediately taken to the Madison hospital, where she died about 15 minutes after her arrival.

Born June 14, 1941 at Huntington Park, Calif., and a former resident of Los Angeles, she would have entered her freshman year at Berlin High School this fall. She was a member of Berlin Methodist Church.

Surviving are her parents; a twin brother. George, a brother, John, and a sister, Jo Ann, all at home; her paternal grandparents, Mr. and Mrs. John Wentland of Berlin and maternal grandparents, Mr. and Mrs. M. L. Webber, Madison.

10

### Rites Thursday

Funeral services will be conducted at 10 a.m. Thursday at Rasque Funeral Home with the Rev. John Francis officiating. Burial will be in Oakwood Cemetery.

Jon McConnell, about 25, of Berlin, was transferred from Berlin Memorial Hospital Saturday afternoon to Wausau, being moved on recommendation from Dr. D. J. Sievers. McConnell was admitted to Berlin Hospital late Friday with a paralyzed bladder condition.

Another 14-year-old, Robin Sanders, son of Mr. and Mrs. Stanley Sanders, who was admitted to Berlin Hospital Thursday for observation, was declared a polio patient today by Dr. Sievers. Sanders has a mild 'bulbar type of the disease and has no sign of paralysis. His condition at present, the doctor said, is good.

One Berlin polio victim, Dennis Schroeder, 14-year-old son of Mr. and Mrs. Elmer Schroeder of Route 3, was returned to his home Sunday by his parents from Wisconsin General Hospital, Madison. He was taken to the latter hospital Thursday, but was released Sunday with his condition reported as a mild case of polio. He will remain at home under observation of Dr. Sievers.

According to Berlin Hospital officials, the weekend wave of polio raised the city's total to five cases. The Wentland girl's death, however, was the first polio fatality in the city this summer.

Mrs. Walker, the mother of our friends, who we had recently played with, was terrified for the safety of her two children. She, with her son Jeffrey, drove to the hospital in Marshfield, Wisconsin, to get gamma globulin for her children. When she arrived at the Berlin Memorial Hospital with the vaccine, she was horrified to be told it could not be used for her children. Instead, Georgie, Jack, and I received double doses of the injection with the hope it would keep us from developing the disease. Gamma globulin is a type of protein located in the plasma of the blood that contains antibodies. The serum is created by combining the gamma globulins from blood donors, and the injections are given in the buttocks to temporarily boost immunity against disease.

The second night after Jeanie's death, the two of us were in bed crying. Georgie said, "I saw Jesus today."

I excitedly asked, "Where?"

"Above Dr. Wiesender's office," he replied, which was across the street from our house. No more was said. As I often recall those four words, I feel Jesus told Georgie he would soon be joining his twin.

Plans were made for Jeanie's funeral, scheduled for Thursday, August 25. My mother and I needed to find clothing for Jeanie to wear ... forever. We searched in the closet that Jeanie and I shared. I wanted Jeanie to wear the precious dress she had just finished sewing but was told it was not appropriate. My mother found a subdued yellow, cotton dress with white trim and cap sleeves. It was a dress neither Jeanie nor I had yet worn, a hand-me-down from our cousin Joyce.

When my parents delivered the clothing to the funeral director, his wife asked for a picture of Jeanie so she could style Jeanie's hair appropriately. She also requested Jeanie's friendship ring to cover the white line on her tan fingers.

# Rites Thursday For Jeanette Wentland, 14, Victim Of Polio

Funeral services were to be held at 10 a.m. Thursday at the Rasque Funeral Home for Jeannette Alice Wentland, 14, daughter of Mr. and Mrs. Harvey Wentland, 109 Spring St., who died at Wisconsin General Hospital Sunday morning of polio.

The Rev. John Francis of the Berlin Methodist Church was to officiate and burial was to be in Oakwood Cemetery.

Miss Wentland was born June 13, 1941, at Huntington Park, Calif., and had lived for a time in Los Angeles. She would have entered her freshman year at Berlin High School this fall. She was a member of the local Methodist Church.

Surviving are her parents; a twin brother, George; a brother, John; and a sister, Jo Ann, all at home; her paternal grandparents, Mr. and Mrs. John Wentland of Berlin, and maternal grandparents, Mr. and Mrs. M. L. Webber of Madison.

Pallbearers were to be two uncles, Myrton and Earl Webber, both of Madison; Rolly Gottbehuet, business associate of her father; and Carl Sprague.

On that same Wednesday, my mother, Jack, and I went to Penney's to find clothing for Jack and me to wear, as we had nothing suitable for the funeral. Georgie was too sick to come with us. Our local JC Penney store, after closing to the public, reopened for our family to shop. We were isolated from the public due to the tremendous fear of the "polio bug" and were grateful for the three clerks who stayed to help us.

Georgie was too sick to attend his twin sister's funeral the next day. The thought of never seeing his twin again was heartbreaking for him. He asked our father to take pictures of her for his keeping. Our father, although not wanting to disappoint him, could not bear to do it.

Rasque Funeral Home was one block from our house. From the corner near our house, I could see adults and children entering and leaving with handkerchiefs in their hands. Our Aunt Ede Webber, from Black Earth, Wisconsin, stayed at our house with Georgie while my parents, Jack, and I walked to our sister's funeral. We were ushered to a private room reserved for the family. Jack and I were led to an area where we could not see the casket. Our aunts and uncles were seated with us and crying after viewing Jeanie. The service was not held in our church for fear of the contagious polio disease.

"You will wish you had seen her. This is your last chance. You will regret you didn't take a final look. I'll go with you." These penetrating words were spoken to me by Mayme, the elderly lady who had previously been our housekeeper and caregiver. Mayme, never having had children, truly cared for us four Wentland children, and she received our affection in return. She was encouraging me to view my sister Jeanie's body in the casket. Neither Jack nor I could bear the heartache of viewing our sister in that state. Mayme, in her caring way, tried to help us. She needed the closure of seeing Jeanie. Our choice and adamant decision was final – we would not walk up to the casket and peer at our dead sister.

| **Services** | **To the Loving Memory of** |
|---|---|
| Held at *Basque Funeral Home* *Berlin, Wis.* | *Jeanie Wentland* |
| Date *August 25, 1955*  Hour *10 a.m.* | Place of birth *Huntington Park, Calif.* |
| CLERGYMAN *Rev. John Francis* | Date *June 13, 1941* |
| | ENTERED INTO REST |
| INTERMENT | |
| Place *Oakwood Cemetery* | Date *August 21, 1955* |
| Section   Block   Lot | |
| City *Berlin* | |
| County *Green Lake* | Place *Berlin, Wisconsin* |
| State *Wisconsin* | |
| Hour *11 a.m.* Day *Thurs.* Month *Aug.* Year *1955* | Age *14* Years *2* Months *8* Days |

Pages from Jeanie's funeral book,
information entered by her mother

After the service, we were led to a large shiny black car – the family car – that followed another shiny black car – the hearse. As we turned the corner passing the park where we often played, I heard the laughter of children. I looked out the large windows and saw children playing. My world had stopped, and I wondered how anyone could be playing at such a sad time.

After returning home from Jeanie's funeral with the relatives, we had a meal. Georgie was not feeling well, but he and I were sitting on our living room sofa talking and playing when we were told to stop making noise. That was the last time we played together.

That evening, Georgie, accompanied by our mother, was taken by ambulance to the Wisconsin General Hospital where he was also diagnosed with bulbar polio. He was given a tracheotomy like his twin sister. Later, my father got a long-distance phone call reporting that Georgie had taken a sudden turn for the worse with a 50-50 chance of survival. On Friday afternoon, Daddy drove to Madison to be with Georgie and Mother. Daddy was optimistic that Georgie would make it but said that Georgie was very afraid.

I was staying with my grandparents in Berlin when my dad came with the minister early Saturday morning to tell us Georgie had died at 5:30 a.m., six days after Jeanie. He took me home while my mother stayed in Madison to complete the necessary paperwork.

# George Wentland, 14, Dies Of Polio; Twin Died 6 Days Ago

## Took Turn For Worse Friday, Died Saturday

George Wentland, 14-year-old son of Mr. and Mrs. Harvey Wentland, 109 Spring St., died of polio at Wisconsin General Hospital, Madison, Saturday morning — just six days after the same disease claimed the life of his twin sister. Death came at 5 a.m.

The boy had been taken to the Madison hospital Thursday evening after doctors were able to definitely diagnose as polio the disease which had seized the boy Tuesday. He was confined in Berlin Memorial Hospital during his sister's funeral Thursday morning.

FRIENDS of the boy's father said Harvey Wentland seemed optimistic about the boy's chances Friday afternoon. But Friday evening a long distance phone call from Madison informed the parents of a sudden turn for the worse, and they left immediately to be by their son's side. They were told then that he had only a 50-50 chance.

Funeral services have not yet been arranged.

DR. A. J. WIESENDER, city health officer, said no other polio cases had been reported this week. In all, six cases had been reported this month, five in Berlin and one just outside the city.

The Wentland twins were the only two fatalities, and three others have been returned home and are on the road to recovery. Jon McConnell remained in Wausau Hospital at last reports.

# Twin of 1st Berlin Polio Fatality Dies

BERLIN — Polio struck a fatal blow to the Harvey Wentland home, 109 Spring St., for the second time in a week as George Wentland, 14, died this morning at Wisconsin General Hospital, Madison.

George was the twin brother of Jeannette Alice Wentland, who died Sunday at Wisconsin General within 15 minutes after being taken there by a Berlin ambulance. She was the first polio death to be recorded in Berlin this summer.

The Wentland boy became ill at his home Tuesday and was unable to attend the Thursday morning funeral of his sister. Thursday evening he was moved to Berlin Hospital, and was transferred to Madison later in the evening on advice of his physician, Dr. D. J. Sievers. The latter described the boy's condition Friday as "possibly bulbar," but final dispostion of the type of polio was not available this morning. He was the city's sixth polio case.

He was born June 14, 1941 at Huntington Park, Calif. and previously lived at Los Angeles, Calif., prior to coming to Berlin. He was to have entered Berlin High School as a freshman this fall, and was a member of Berlin Methodist Church.

Surviving are his parents; a brother, John, and a sister, Jo Ann, all at home; paternal grandparents, Mr. and Mrs. John Wentland of Berlin, and maternal grandparents, Mr. and Mrs. M. L. Webber of Madison.

Funeral arrangements are incomplete.

Later that same day, my brother, Jack, became sick and my dad rode with Jack to the hospital in Madison. Enroute the ambulance passed the car returning my mother home following Georgie's death.

When the car with two men and my mother pulled into our driveway, I ran out the back door to meet her. As she got out of the car, I announced, "They just took Jack!" Mother yelled out, "Oh no!"

Again, Jack's diagnosis was polio.

18

# Rites Set For Second Polio Victim

BERLIN — Funeral services were set for Tuesday afternoon for George Wentland, 14, the second member of the Harvey Wentland family to succumb from polio.

His twin sister, Jeanette, died at a Madison hospital Aug. 21. George, who began feeling ill before Jeanette's funeral, was taken to the Madison hospital Friday suffering from the bulbar type of poliomyelitis. He died early Saturday.

The Rev. John Francis will officiate at the services at the Rasque Funeral Home at 2 p.m. Interment will be in Oakwood Cemetery.

Surviving, in addition to his parents, are a brother, John, and a sister, JoAnn, and his grandparents, Mr. and Mrs. John Wentland, Berlin, and Mr. and Mrs. M. L. Webber, Madison.

George Wentland was born June 13, 1941, in Huntington Park, Calif., and had lived here the past several years. He was graduated from the eighth grade at Washington School last June.

Three days after Jeanie's funeral, my mother and I needed to find clothing for Georgie to wear . . . forever. In his closet, we found a suit, shirt, and tie that had fit him fairly well and were also passed down from a friend. It was at this time I heard how a funeral director dressed the bodies in preparation for showing. I was sad to hear that the clothing was cut "up the back" and wrapped around the body just for showing. I wanted Georgie to wear shoes but was tersely told "it isn't necessary."

At that time I began to realize how helpless my dear siblings were. They were no longer alive, not able to dress themselves, and the three of us would never again share our secrets, our stories, or our love.

## John Wentland Holds His Own In Polio Bout

John Wentland, 16, son of Mr. and Mrs. Harvey Wentland, 109 Spring St., the third member of the family to be stricken with polio, was reported in "good" condition at University Hospital, Madison, where he was taken Saturday afternoon.

His father said Tuesday that the boy's fever is slowly being brought down. Although his condition is not believed to be serious, his father said no one could predict how long he would be confined.

John's twin brother and sister, George and Jeanette, 14, died last week, both victims of polio. A fourth child of the Harvey Wentlands, JoAnn, 11, is at home and has not contracted the disease.

Local health officials reported no new cases in the city over the weekend.

## Funeral Tuesday For Polio Victim, George Wentland

Funeral services were held Tuesday afternoon for George Wentland, 14, second member of the Harvey Wentland family to succumb to polio.

George died at Wisconsin General Hospital, Madison, Saturday at 5 a.m. His twin sister, Jeanette, died at the same hospital six days earlier.

The Rev. John Francis officiated at services Tuesday afternoon at the Rasque Funeral Home. Interment was in Oakwood Cemetery.

Besides his parents, George is survived by a brother, John, who is now in Wisconsin General Hospital suffering from polio; a sister, JoAnn; and his grandparents, Mr. and Mrs. John Wentland, Berlin, and Mr. and Mrs. M. L. Weber, Madison.

George Wentland was born in Huntington Park, Calif., June 13, 1941, and had lived in Los Angeles before coming to Berlin several years ago. He graduated from the eighth grade at Washington School last spring and was to have entered Berlin High School as a freshman this fall.

Don Rasque, the funeral director, and his wife were friends of our family and had no children of their own. I recalled Mr. Rasque sitting with us on the street curb one day, talking, teasing, and laughing. We enjoyed seeing this happy, playful man who was always ready to say a few words to us. He shared his feelings with my father after their funerals, saying that Jeanie's and Georgie's funerals were the most difficult he had to officiate. Don and his wife Mabel had difficulty hiding the suture lines along both kids' hairlines from their autopsies. He added that he would leave the funeral business if he was ever in another similar situation.

Back at home, my parents were faced with another funeral. Georgie's funeral was held three days after he died. They hurriedly made the arrangements as time was needed to be with Jack who was now also stricken.

Only three of us took the second walk to the funeral home this time, on Tuesday, August 30. Jack was now in the Wisconsin General Hospital in Madison. My parents and I again were ushered to the room reserved for the family where our aunts and uncles were, again, seated and crying. I took the same seat I sat in five days previous. And again, I chose not to see my sibling in his casket, but heard from those who viewed both of them as to how "peaceful they looked – as if they were asleep." I didn't want to see them asleep; I wanted to see them awake and alive.

| To the Loving Memory of | Services |
|---|---|

*To the Loving Memory of*

GEORGIE WENTLAND

Place of birth HUNTINGTON PARK, CALIF.

Date JUNE 14, 1941

ENTERED INTO REST

Date AUGUST 27, 1955

Place BERLIN, WISCONSIN

Age 14 Years 2 Months 14 Days

*Services*

Held at BASQUE FUNERAL HOME
BERLIN, WIS.

Date AUGUST 30, 1955    Hour 10 A.m.

CLERGYMAN

REV. JOHN FRANCIS

INTERMENT

Place OAKWOOD CEMETERY

Section    Block    Lot

City BERLIN,

County GREEN LAKE

State WISCONSIN

Hour 11 a.m. Day TUES. Month Aug. Year 1955

Pages from Georgie's funeral book,
information entered by his mother

The service ended, and we were, again, led to the shiny black family car waiting for us, with the hearse ahead. As the car slowly drove away, I saw Georgie's Boy Scout Troup #32 in uniform, standing at attention, their right hands saluting. Mr. Thalacker, their Scoutmaster, was at the front of the long line of boys, holding a flag. Jeffrey, one of the scouts and a playmate of Georgie and me, still at attention, waved his left hand slightly when our eyes met. The Boy Scout Troup #32 was also standing

22

at attention at Georgie's open gravesite next to his twin sister Jeanie.

As we passed the park, children, again, were at play. Didn't they realize the world had stopped?!

Years later, my mother mentioned that glass covered their open caskets for health reasons. The fear of the dreaded disease discouraged people from attending the funerals. Family members from Woodruff, Wisconsin, did not attend the funeral because of their fear. And our Madison cousins, Jan, Judy, Pat, and Laurie were not allowed to attend for the same reason. Dennis, a 12-year-old neighbor, told of being afraid to go to sleep at night fearing he would die as he slept.

No one knew for sure how polio was transmitted or how it selected its victims. However, polio outbreaks followed the circus traveling the Midwest. At this time, the cause was thought to be from animal waste with flies as the vehicle. My mother and I always felt this way. For years my mother would go berserk when she would see a fly in our house.

Things were happening so fast I don't remember thinking how I was feeling. I don't remember feeling I may get sick and die. Even though I lost my two favorite friends, I "kinda" felt they would come back. Never having experienced the death of anyone, the loss of Jeanie and Georgie was something for which I was not prepared. It happened so quickly. Our home was in constant turmoil: telephone calls, newspaper articles, funeral plans, articles of clothing, what should Jeanie wear, what about Georgie, Jack not feeling well, flowers, cemetery plots, caskets and

23

vaults, Jack in the hospital, cards and letters coming in, thank you cards going out. I helped my mother with thank you cards and noticed I placed the stamp on the wrong corner on some of the envelopes. When mailing them and talking to the postmaster, he said to not worry; he would gladly hand-cancel them.

Visitors to the house were few as people were afraid of the "polio bug." Dishes of food were placed on the sidewalk in front of our house. Neighbors directly across the street brought us two pies, and several warm casserole dishes were left on the porch by our back door. We wondered if the people wanted their dishes returned. Mrs. Walker, the mother of Georgie's friend Jeffrey, asked Jeffrey what Georgie's favorite food was. His 12-year-old friend exclaimed, "Watermelon!" So Mrs. Walker placed a large watermelon on our front porch.

Best friends, Georgie on left, and Jeffrey

Churches offered prayers, and collections were taken for our family. Love and care were shown by many in Berlin. My parents smiled when they heard collections were taken in local taverns. The money helped as my parents did not have life insurance on their children. My mother was thankful we didn't have a "quarantine sign slapped on the front door of our house" in addition to interviewers arriving from the television stations.

I had shared a room and bed with Jeanie and was not able to sleep alone, even with the help of sleeping pills prescribed by our doctor. After Jeanie died, I immediately joined Georgie in his bed. During our four nights together, we cried, prayed, and shared our thoughts and feelings. This was sibling love between a 12-year-old sister and a 14-year-old brother sharing the horrific loss of our sister.

After Georgie died, I began sleeping with a light on in my parents' room. When they went to bed, they would move me to Georgie's bed. I never returned to the spacious room Jeanie and I shared. I felt more secure in Georgie's small room. I remember awaking many mornings, pinching my eyes tightly closed, hoping the horror was just a bad dream. With my eyes closed and my hands folded across my waist, I would sometimes lie there picturing them in their caskets. I felt I was with them, one on either side. This was a comfort to me.

We were a church-going family of six, and we all loved our minister. After the twins' deaths, the minister told my mother that if she would have taken them to a chiropractor, the chiropractor could have saved them. How awful to have said such a thing! At a later date, he apologized to my mother for that remark.

The ambulance took Jack to the same hospital in Madison in the afternoon of the day our brother Georgie died. Mother had ridden in the ambulance with Georgie and when Georgie took a turn for the worse the following day, Daddy drove to Madison to be with Georgie and Mother.

When Georgie died at 5:30 that morning, Daddy returned to Berlin, picked up our minister Reverend Francis, and drove to my Grandpa and Grandma Wentland's house where I was staying. That's when he announced to us that Georgie had died. I couldn't believe it was true. My Grandpa and Grandma Wentland, my father, Reverend Francis, and I joined in prayer.

Daddy took me home where he found how sick Jack was. This time Daddy rode in the ambulance with Jack.

At the hospital, Jack was given some of the same life-saving procedures that his siblings received. He did not have a tracheotomy but was packed in ice to lower his temperature. He was in intensive care for several days until his temperature began to fall. Jack was terrified. He thought he was going to die, like his siblings, or be crippled. He wondered if it was his turn. The doctors told my mother they did all they could to save his life and added, "He is in the hands of God." Those profound words were important for me to hear and helped me in my faith in God.

## Another From Berlin Family Polio Patient

BERLIN — John Wentland, 16, son of Mr. and Mrs. Harvey Wentland, 109 Spring St., the third member of the family to be stricken with polio, was reported in "good" condition at University Hospital, Madison, where he was taken Saturday afternoon.

Reports reaching here indicated there was some paralysis of the youth's limbs, but the severity of the disease was not known.

John's twin brother and sister, George and Jeanette, 14, died last week, both victims of polio. A fourth child of the Harvey Wentlands, JoAnn, 11, is at home and has not contacted the disease.

Local health officials reported no new cases in the city over the weekend.

When his condition improved, Jack was moved into a large ward with other polio victims where he spent time in an iron lung, a type of respirator that encloses the patient - except for the head - in an airtight container. The air pressure in the iron lung is decreased and increased with a mechanical diaphragm to replace the action of the patient's paralyzed diaphragm. Some patients were destined to stay in the iron lung for the remainder of their lives. Jack witnessed other children in iron lungs and rocking beds and worried about what would happen to them if the electricity went out. He wrote letters home, threatening to break out, and sent them "air mail," even though Madison was only 80 miles away. He asked for his Bible.

Jack had been in the hospital several days when I asked my mother, "Is everything going to be okay?" She gave me a hug and assured me, "Yes." I think back to asking that question as to how could everything be okay when so much that was not okay had already happened. It hurts me to imagine my brother, just before his 16th birthday, riding in the ambulance after seeing his younger sister and brother go through the same process and die.

While my parents visited Jack, I stayed at my Grandma Webber's home in Madison and missed the opening of school. My dad, who was back at work in Berlin, would bring me letters from my friends. I enjoyed reading their friendly and encouraging words. A letter from Shari told me to "keep your chin up." I often recall those four words from my 12-year-old friend. Grandma would sometimes accidentally call me Jeanie, and I would say, "I'm Jo." She would reply, "I am so used to having Jeanie in the kitchen. Jeanie was always a good helper." I felt my grandma wished I would have died instead of Jeanie, and I felt I was always in the way.

On one visit, my parents brought Jack's girlfriend Judie and me to the hospital. We could see Jack through a glass door, and he walked up to it to talk to us. Judie, in her sweet voice pleaded, "Now, Johnny, you have to get better." (I think she was the only one who called him Johnny.) That visit was a big boost to his recovery. Judie's parents also drove her to visit him at a time when he could go outside. She said they wanted to kiss and were able to "sneak one in."

My mother had instructions from the Berlin Health Department to sanitize the walls and floors in our entire home. My father showed me a "new way to do dishes." His words came out slowly and softly as he said "we no longer dry them with a towel." As he walked over to the stove, he picked up the tea kettle filled with boiling water, returned to the sink, and poured the boiling water over the washed dishes.

Berlin took immediate precautions to avoid the spreading of the disease. Some parents kept their children in their own yards and requested a rest time each day to strengthen their resistance. Crowds were avoided, scheduled carnivals and county fairs were cancelled. Public swimming pools and beaches were closed and playing in parks was discouraged. Some surrounding areas delayed the starting of schools.

Bill, a child raised in a neighboring city, remembers attending theater movies after the banning of some public places was discontinued. An advertisement on the screen asked everyone to give a dime for the March of Dimes collection instead of buying themselves a treat. The advertisement showing children lying in iron lungs and walking with braces on their legs touched his heart as he donated his dime.

In addition, to this day I am amazed at what people say in tragic situations like that. I overheard a woman telling my mother that it was a shame that Jeanie never had the chance to experience sex. One of my eighth grade classmates told me I was "hard-hearted" because she didn't ever see me cry. A distant relative remarked that my parents came out ahead because of the insurance money. How callous! My parents not only didn't have insurance, but how can you trade money for the lives of your children? Two years after the deaths of our siblings, an aunt visiting our family asked Jack if he would drive her to the cemetery to visit his sister's and brother's graves. Jack had a car of his own and obliged. When the two of them were standing at the graves, she said to him, "Now aren't you sorry you were so mean to them?" I never heard Jack mention this. My aunt told me what she did. I don't remember my response; however, I'm sure I was too shocked at her lack of consideration. She apparently missed the opportunity of seeing the four of us having fun together at play.

Before we moved from Spring Street, I stayed at school until late to avoid going to an empty house. I walked to the Walker Insurance Agency where my mother worked and rode home with her. I also avoided walking past the double doors at the funeral home where the hearse was parked. This practice lasted through my high school years.

## BEGGARS' NIGHT: OUR FIRST VISITOR

The end of October was exhilarating to our family. Jack would soon be returning home from the hospital after a two-month stay in the polio ward. No more isolation and no more panic and fear while waiting for the day he would return. All four of us were elated; nothing else of importance was on our minds.

For two months, after polio invaded our home, we never heard a knock at our front door nor did anyone attempt to step inside. We were finally making strides to return to a semblance of a normal life.

On the evening of October 30, we heard a noise on our front steps and porch. My father and I answered the loud banging on the door. When we opened it, we saw a large boy standing alone with an open pillow case. He shouted, "Trick or Treat!"

My father, caught off guard, began to respond, "I'm sorry. We aren't prepared. Jack is coming home from the hospital…" As he was trying to explain, the boy reached into his pocket, pulled out a hunk of wax and drew large marks on our glass storm door. The haunting sound of the wax hitting and being drawn across the glass halted my dad's speech. The boy loudly stomped off the porch. My dad turned to me and, in his quiet yet deliberate voice said, "And that stuff is hard to clean off."

Beggars' Night was another night of trick-or-treating practiced by a

31

few kids in Berlin. The following night was for the traditional Halloween trick-or-treating and we were ready.

Recalling this particular event has not been easy for me, as it happened at the time when my family was anticipating our first positive experience since losing the twins. I now wonder if the one "trickster" who visited 109 Spring Street on Beggars' Night didn't know he was at the house that was "filled with polio germs." Did he ever realize the effect and possible consequences of his loud banging on the door at that particular house or have any clue as to the family's devastation that had occurred just two months prior?

# CHRISTMAS 1955

My mother was determined we would not spend Christmas 1955 in the house that became too large and too full of sad memories. My parents found a small house to rent that was several blocks away. Our family of four moved into the small three-bedroom house on State Street shortly before Christmas. My small bedroom was in the center of the house where I felt more secure.

My parents, Jeanette and Harvey, at their home on State Street

33

I spent that first Christmas day at my boyfriend Allen's house. I thought my being away on that day was helpful to my parents; however, now I think differently. Jack wasn't home that day either. My parents were alone on Christmas Day 1955 for the first time in 17 years, alone without their four children, two of whom would never spend another Christmas day with them.

## MOTHER'S CHRISTMAS LETTER OF 1955

*Berlin, Wisconsin*
*January 1956*
*Dear*

*Because so many of you have written us and because so many of you thought of us during the holiday season, Harvey and I have decided this is the best means of letting you know how we are doing without taking a whole year to write each one of you individually.*

*We know you are wondering about our John (Jackie, to many of you). He is coming along 100%. 'Tis a slow pace for a 16-year-old, but the important fact is that he will be okay in time. He started back to school after Thanksgiving vacation and at this time he has "caught up" with his class. When he first came home he went to Oshkosh (20 miles from Berlin), three times a week for therapy. At present he goes twice a week and before too long they tell us he can get along with only one treatment a week. He gets physical therapy and occupational therapy; the occupational therapy treatment is for use of his hands, arms, and shoulders. You see, his bout with polio was a combination of the bulbar type and the non-paralytic type; he isn't crippled in any way but has decided weakness in the muscles of the arms, shoulders, and hands. There are times when he has difficulty with breathing, but that comes with excitement and we are told that he, no doubt, will always have that trouble. He wasn't able to do any hunting this fall and that was a big*

34

disappointment to both him and his dad. Ice fishing hasn't been too good for Jack either, because as soon as his hands get cold, he's done for. With a whole year ahead of him now, we are sure that next fall and winter he will be able to do all the things he enjoys.

After seven years in one house, the Wentlands moved – and just at Christmas time. We managed to get ourselves just comfortably settled before the holidays and we didn't have the time to send a card or write anyone. Both Harvey and I kept up with our jobs during the moving process so I am sure you all will understand why time was such a big factor. Now that we have made the move, we are glad we did it, when we did. We didn't have time to think; we were too busy and tired. Jack and Jo Ann weren't a bit enthused about Christmas until just a few days before it arrived. Our spirits – all 4 of us – were at a low ebb. But as Jack and Jo Ann began to get the "feeling," so did Harvey and I and we did have a nice day.

I know most of you would like a quick run-down on our new house. We found one (to rent) that is just a dream; all on one floor, 3 bedrooms, dining room, living room, kitchen and bath with a full basement. This is the first time since we left the West Coast that we have lived in a house, all by ourselves, with the exception of 6 months that we lived in Spring Lake; perhaps you can sense our elation. We have a beautiful big yard, loads of flowers, birds, and a nice big garden space. At this time I have about decided to give up fishing next summer in order to take care of the yard and gardening. We are only a block from the Fox River and maybe I can find enough time to keep in practice during the walleye season at least!

Jo Ann is fine; she's such a busy girl at school this year, we wonder what she will do in high school next fall. She likes sports, all the social functions, and has just oodles of friends. She sure is a big girl for her 13 years; tall and slender. She's beginning to fill out now and is so happy that her friends don't call her "bean pole" anymore. She has had two Salk *shots and will get her third and last shot in May. She is a very nervous youngster, but we all can understand why. All of us have had a terrific adjustment to make and I know you all will understand us when we say it isn't easy.*

*We are humbly grateful that God has somehow given us the strength to keep our heads up and keep us going. We are humbly grateful to each and every one of you, too, for your thoughtfulness during these past months. Your kind thoughts and prayers have meant more to us than words can ever tell.*

---------

When reading this Christmas letter, many years later, I realized my mother never mentioned the death of the twins. I wonder if she was feeling those same thoughts I felt for so many years. Was it too devastating and heartbreaking to write about the horrific tragedy our family endured?

After the sicknesses and deaths, my parents and I tried attending church. We would sit in the rear pew and leave the church as soon as we began crying. My mom and dad simply could not attend church anymore. After time, I returned to church and became active again. Several years later, I became the church secretary. My parents, I believe, kept their faith. My dad read the Bible daily and my mother had a special prayer book that showed significant wear.

# SCHOOL PORTRAITS

Having a yearly photograph taken is an important day in a child's school year. Clothing is meticulously chosen, a haircut is appropriate, and an attractive smile is practiced in preparation for the scheduled photo session.

In the fall of 1954, the twins, Georgie and Jeanie, started eighth grade at Washington School. Soon after school began, a date was scheduled for yearly pictures. Mr. Carter, a local photographer, who was dependable, punctual, and professional, was selected. He was particular in how his equipment was set up, even to the point of measuring the distance each child sat from the camera. A string attached to the front of his camera was stretched to each child's nose, creating a bit of giggling which he captured on film.

The completed packets of black and white prints were delivered to school after the developing and printing process. Each packet contained a price list for the various purchase options. My family ordered the usual one 5" x 7", several smaller sizes for relatives, and most often, all the 1½" x 2½" sizes for trading with friends.

Since our parents didn't buy the largest 8" x 10" size photo plus several of the smaller options, we would return unpurchased photos in the packets. The Carter Studio saved these packets for one year after which they were discarded one by one into the furnace. Mr. Carter told my mother he was ready to toss the envelope containing Georgie's photos when he recognized his freckled face through the cellophane. The next photo packet in the stack was of Jeanie, his twin sister.

Mr. Carter kindly saved the two most important pictures that could have been so easily discarded and lost forever. His wife Lois, who helped at their studio, oil-colored the two 8" x 10" portraits and presented them to our family. For many years, the priceless gift from the Carter family was displayed in a folding double frame in our living room and still remains a treasured gift.

People in our community, knowing Mr. Carter wore a "big built-up shoe," never questioned his conspicuous limp and short, withered leg. He too was a victim of polio as a child.

# "In Memoriam"

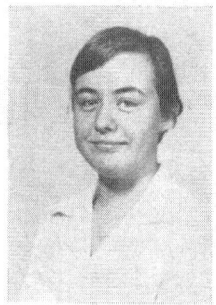

Jeanette and George Wentland

## IN MEMORY

The staff of the 1956 Mascoutin feels that it is fitting that its yearbook should pay tribute to two students who might have shared in and been a part of the many activities which are reviewed in this book.

Jeanette and George Wentland, victims of the fatal polio epidemic that struck during the summer of 1955, would have been members of the freshman class this year. Those who knew George and Jean will certainly miss having them to share their high school activities. We are sure that these two students would have been an important asset to our high school.

A page from the school yearbook, The Mascoutin

# JEANIE'S DIARY

The word "love" is defined in Webster's Dictionary as "a feeling of strong personal attachment." This portrays my affection for my sister Jeanie. We were roommates, playmates, friends, and occasional enemies. Seventeen months older, she was most often my mentor.

Georgie and Grandpa would have a ball going to the city dump to find treasures. They would search through the rubble and find a lot of useful things. That's where Georgie found the diary he gave to Jeanie.

Our mother was not a saver. She enforced an uncluttered, tidy, clean home with everything in its place. It is a mystery to me that for the past 42 years, my sister Jeanie's small, black diary had been preserved where I found it among our mother's few safeguarded keepsakes.

As I opened the small book, the first penciled words made me chuckle, "Stay out, Jo (Nosey)." Reflecting on my age 12 and her age 13, Jeanie's entry was most appropriate.

The next page, the one recording the important and identifying facts such as name, address, phone number, as well as height and weight, were completed in full: Weight - 107, Height - 5 feet, Color of Hair - brown, and Color of Eyes - green; In Case of Emergency, Notify - Gambles or Walker Agency. With the preliminaries completed, she was ready to write in her daily journal.

On January 1, she had written, "I got this diary March 16 so I couldn't write in it. I will write jokes and songs that are my favorite." January 2, "Knock! Knock! Who's there? Weasel. Weasel who? Weasel while you work." Holding true to her promise to write jokes, the next entry reads, "What did one tonsil say to the other tonsil? Better get dressed. Doctor's taking us out tonight." Then she continued with her favorite songs.

I surmise she ran out of jokes and favorite songs because the following pages are blank until March 10 when she wrote "Are you friend or enema?" Then, skipping a few days, the entry on March 14 reads, "We played basketball. We won 50 to 32. I made 2 baskets and 1 free throw total 5."

The year 1955 appears at the top of the page dated March 16, where she wrote, "Georgie gave me this diary."

I began to laugh as I vividly recalled the event of her next entry. She wrote, "I got in a fight with Jo. I beat the shit out of her. I promised myself I will not talk to her for a week or over. I did talk to her at 7:30. Grandma had a heart attack. She is better."

I remember that fight – not necessarily what it was about, but the activity that transpired in our bedroom. Jeanie pinned me on our bed, put my pillow over my face, and hit me in the eyes. That was the one time I actually saw stars! I cried, and, yes, her diary revealed it accurately: she beat the shit out of me. Our fight, most likely, had something to do with cleaning or re-arranging the furniture in our shared bedroom, a source of common disagreements.

Her diary continues with notes of seeing friends at school, listening to the radio, shopping, going to the movies, watching TV, cleaning the house, and washing and ironing the family's weekly laundry. On March 25, she wrote, "Cynitha (sic) came over for supper. We went to movie. Jo saw Jackie kissing Judy." Jackie was our 15-year-old brother.

At the end of March, Jim's name began appearing daily. Later she wrote, "had loads of fun with Jim. Do not like him." I knew she had a crush on Jim, a boy who would also be entering his first year of high school in the fall. As I continued reading, I found her diary typical of a 13-year-old eighth-grade girl.

Because this gifted diary had a misprint on the days and months that followed, Jeanie corrected the days and dates as she journaled until April 10, Easter morning. As I paged forward searching for more of her precious words, I noticed June 13 was missing Georgie and Jeanie's 14th – and last – birthdays.

My heart raced as I turned to the last entry Jeanie had made in correcting the date: August 20. After taking a deep breath, I slowly turned the page that should have been corrected to read August 21. That date and all others following remained uncorrected and blank. She died on August 21, 1955.

Did she have a reason to stop her entries on what was to become the last full day of her life, or was this powerful 3" x 4" black book preserved 42 years for her sister to find, read, enjoy, share, and reflect on a possible prophecy? For, on August 6, she wrote one single word, "Decided." I wonder what she decided or what was decided for her.

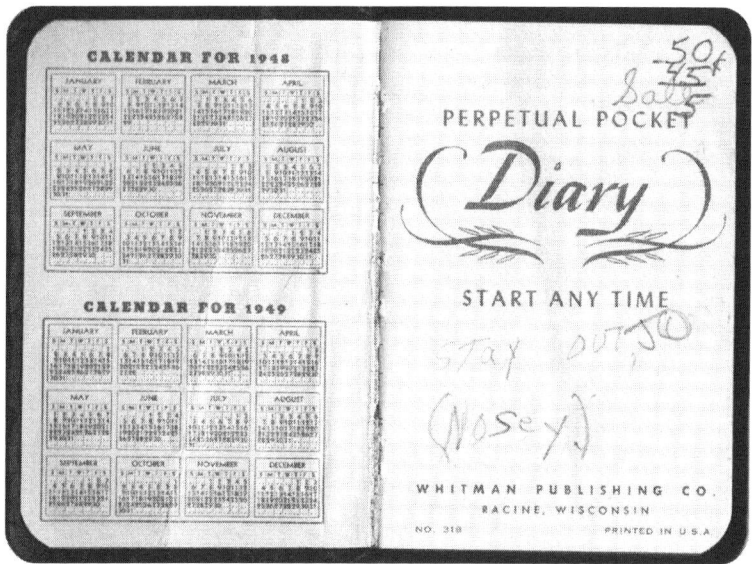

Jo Ann Wentland Koch

Left:
Name: Jeannie Wentland
Residence Address: 109 S Spring St
Phone: 372-M
Business Address: Washington School
My weight is 107, Height 5 feet
Color of hair: brown, Color of eyes: green
In case of emergency please notify: Gambles or Walker Agency
Automobile License No. E-9324
Valuable Papers are at: Journal

Right:
January 1: I got this diary Mar. 16 So I couldn't write in it.
I will write jokes & songs that are my favorite.
January 2: Knock! Knock! Who's there? Weasel. Weasel who?
Weasel while you work.
January 3: What did one tonsil say to the other tonsil?
Better get dressed. Doctor's taking us out tonight.

44

Left:
January 4: *"Wedding Bells!" "Davy Crokett!" "Sincerly" "Melody of Love"*
January 5: *Roses are red violets are blue, pigs stink and so does cows.*
*(Har de Har)*
January 6: *Don't get wise*

Left:
*March 10: Are you friend or enima?*

Right:
*March 14: We played basketball. We won 50 to 32.*
*I made 2 baskets and 1 free throw total 5.*

Left:
*March 16: George gave me this diary. I*
*stated the book "A Man for March." I got a letter from Romelle.*
*Played ring tennis.*
*March 17: I got in a fight with Jo. I beat the shit out of her.*
*I promised myself I will not talk to her for a week or over.*
*I did talk to her at 7:30. Grandma had a heart attack. She is better.*
*March 18: We had a game (won). Grandma is better.*
*Laughed all day. No school. I got a dollar for cleaning.*
*I bought a ring.*

Right:
*March 19: I cleaned upstairs. Changed room around. Just like spring.*
*Wore jacket. I got library book. Read. Grandma better!*
*Got box from Nina jewelry.*
*March 20: Washed (not much) watched TV. Don & Jean came over.*
*Played cards. Jo went to movie. Snowed out.*
*March 21: First day of spring! It snowed. Very wet.*
*Had fun with Jim. Wrote notes & played ping pong. Lost with Alvera!*

Left:
*March 22: Snowed in Monday night. About 12 in.*
*No school in afternoon. Went over to Di's with Judy & Sam.*
*Went to movie "Young at Heart."*
*March 23: Went to school. Stopped snowing.*
*Played ring tennis (won). Listen to radio at night.*
*Sat next to Jim in school movie. Had fun with him.*
*March 24: After school went to game. Kept care of lights.*
*Watch TV Climax & Ford Theater. Rory Calhoun (wow).*

Right:
*March 25: Cynitha came over for supper. We went to movie.*
*Jo saw Jackie kissing Judy. Don't like Jim very much.*
*March 26: Cleaned upstairs. Washed hair. Washed cloths.*
*Watched TV lhilty till 11: Joan Bennett. Played in snow.*
*March 27: Took bath in morning. Listen to radio.*
*Ironed and went for ride.*

Left:
*March 28: Quite warm. Lost my ring. Gave my dec.*
*Found my ring in bed. Happy now, real happy.*
*March 29: Had load of fun with Jim. Do not like him.*
*Real nice outside. Watched TV.*
*March 30: Bad day. Everything went wrong.*
*Didn't wear coat to school a (little ways). Clarnce came over. Ring tennis.*
*Went outside & played in water.*

Right:
*March 31: Last day of school for awhile. Got our report cards.*
*I did pretty good.*
*April 1: No school. Went to Fond du Lac. Had loads of fun.*
*At night went to home show.*
*April 2: Cleaned upstairs in morning. Went to home show.*
*Got new jacket. Wore shorts upstairs.*

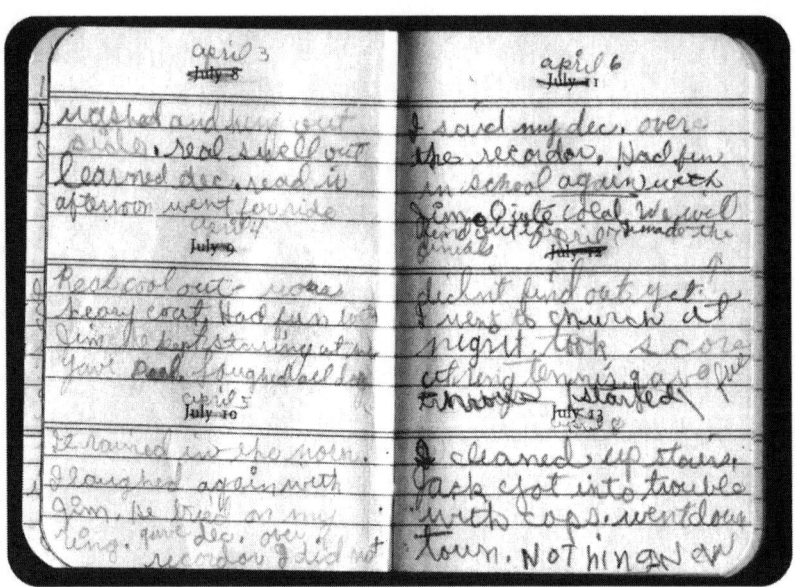

Left:
*April 3: Washed & hung outside. Real swell out. Learned dec.*
*Read in afternoon. Went for ride.*
*April 4: Real cool out. Wore heavy coat. Had fun with Jim.*
*He kept staring at me. Gave ?. Laughed all day.*
*April 5: It rained in the morn. I laughed again with Jim.*
*He tried on my ring. Gave dec over recorder. I did not.*

Right:
*April 6: I said my dec. over the recorder.*
*Had fun in school again with Jim. Quite cold.*
*We will find out if I made the finals.*
*April 7: Didn't find out yet. I went to church at night.*
*Took score at ring tennis. Gave free throws (started).*
*April 8: I cleaned upstairs. Jack got into trouble with cops.*
*Went downtown. Nothing new.*

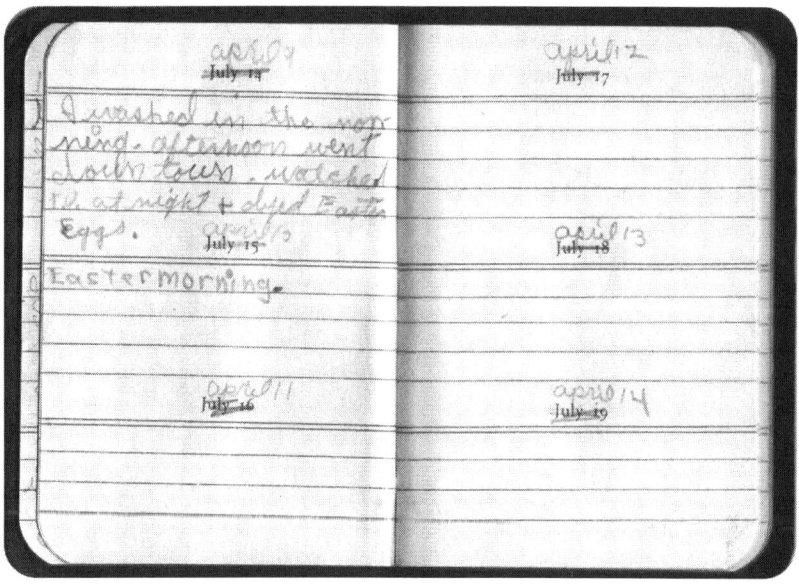

Left:
*April 9: I washed in the morning. Afternoon went downtown.
Watched TV at night & dyed Easter eggs.
April 10: Easter morning.*

Right:
*August 6: Decided.*

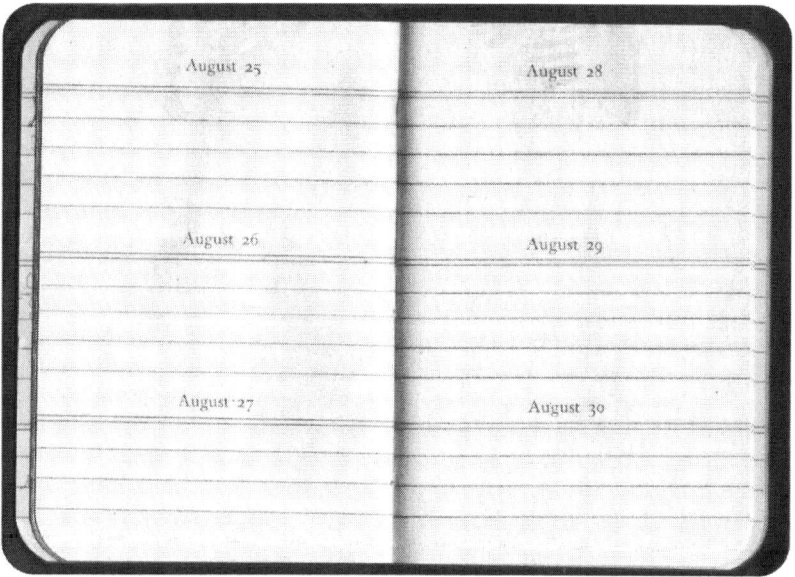

I noticed when reading the names of visitors in Jeanie's and Georgie's funeral books that "Jim" had signed each of their books. It was the same Jim who was mentioned so often in Jeanie's diary.

The friendship ring Jeanie mentioned in her diary . . .

- on March 18 when she made the purchase,
- March 28 when she lost it and was happy when she later found it in bed,
- April 5 she recorded Jim tried her ring on his finger . . .

was special to my sister from the day she bought it. She wore it daily until her death. This is the ring the funeral director's wife requested Jeanie wear to cover the white line on her tan fingers.

Jeanie and her eighth-grade friends - Spring 1955
Left to right: Diana Walker, Jeanie, Judy Parsons, Sara Anderson

# THE EARLY YEARS

*Jo Ann Wentland Koch*

## MY PARENTS MAKE A PLEDGE

On September 10, 1938, Harvey Edward Wentland and Jeanette Alice Webber became Mr. and Mrs. Harvey E. Wentland in the Chapel of the Hills, Hollywood, California. That special day began a pledge – "In sickness and in health, until death do us part" – that lasted their entire lives. The 27-year-old groom and 24-year-old bride were a couple in love with dreams of building a home, raising a family, and living "happily ever after."

A western wedding...Unless our memory and the movie magazines have failed us, the Rev. Neal Dodd, who performed the marriage ceremony of Jeanette Webber and Harvey Wentland Saturday evening in Hollywood, Calif., is none other than the tall, dignified person who appears in practically all movie weddings as the officiating clergyman...Jeanette Webber is the daughter of Mr. and Mrs. Merton La Monte Webber, 1160 Emerald st., and her wedding took place in the St. Mary of the Angels church in Hollywood.

*Jo Ann Wentland Koch*

# Miss Jeanette Webber Weds Harvey Wentland in Hollywood Church

In the St. Mary of the Angel church, Hollywood, Calif., Miss Jeanette Alice Webber, daughter of Mr. and Mrs. Merton La Monte Webber, 1160 Emerald st., was married Saturday night to Harvey Edward Wentland, Los Angeles, son of Mr. and Mrs. John Wentland, Coloma. The Rev. Neal Dodd performed the ceremony.

Miss Webber wore a white mousseline de soie gown with a Queen Anne collar and a long train with insertions of Chantilly lace. Her long tulle veil, bordered with wide bands of Chantilly lace, fell in graceful folds from a Tudor cap studded with seed pearls. She carried tea roses and sweet peas.

The bride was attended by Mrs. J. H. Anderson, sister of the bridegroom, and Mr. Anderson was the best man. Mrs. Anderson wore a pink lace gown over taffeta and a pink tulle hat. Her flowers were white roses and sweet peas.

A reception for 20 guests was held at the Anderson home in Los Angeles after the ceremony. Among those present was Mrs. M. L. Webber, Madison, mother of the bride.

The bride is a graduate of West igh school and of the Groves-arnhart school for secretaries.

58

Harvey and Jeanette at their one-year anniversary

Harvey and Jeanette became Daddy and Mommy one year later when John Harvey was born, fulfilling their first dream of becoming parents. My mother had complications in both pre- and post-delivery. I never heard what the complications were; only that it was a dangerous natural birth using instruments. My mother also cried when she couldn't nurse her baby and could see him only once a day while they were in the hospital. My dad saw his son through a glass window for a few minutes every evening. Over one week passed and the new mommy and son were healthy enough to go home.

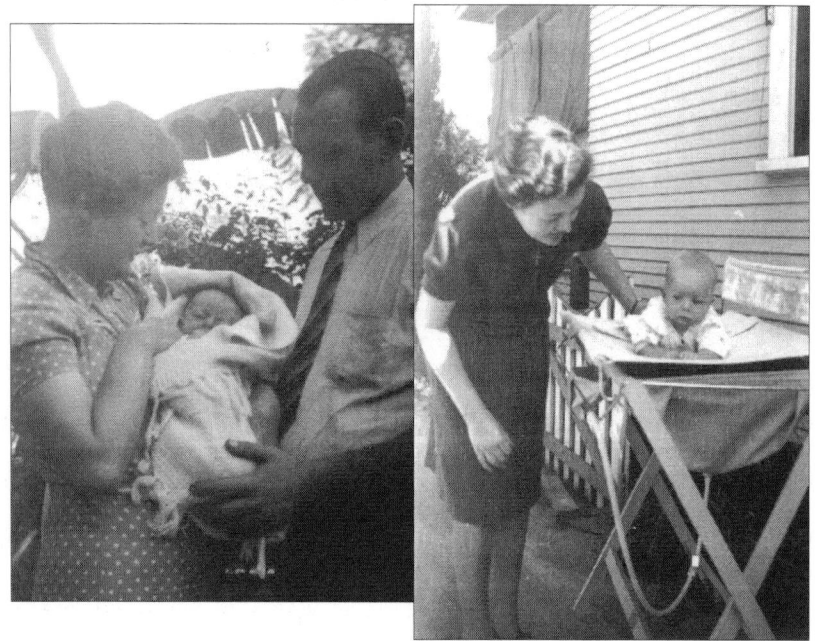

Baby Jackie – 1939

My mother corresponded with my aunt about maybe having Alice Jean in a few years, and they would then have their one boy and their one girl. The history of the name Jeanette Alice began with Alice Jean many generations previous, and the generations would go back and forth with the girl names.

Baby John was nicknamed "Jackie" right away. My mom always had special feelings for her first child and said only that "he was sick as a baby." However, after infancy, he was a normal, happy, healthy child. My mother and Jack always had a special bond.

My dad drew a plan for his dream house: a typical California house,

U-shaped with a garden yard in the center. The plans were never used but remained among treasured belongings. He was employed at the Standard Oil Company when he suffered his first heart attack. He wasn't able to return to his job as he suffered a second heart attack the day he was to return to work. His drinking habits escalated and he became an active binge drinker.

On June 13, 1941, the twins were born. My dad was on one of his drinking binges when my mother went to the hospital to have, what she thought was, her second baby. During the delivery, she heard the doctor say, "Here's another one in there." Neither she nor her doctor knew she was carrying twins. Before my mother could go home with her two new babies, she had to name them. Without her husband, she decided to name the girl Jeanette Alice after herself and the boy George Webber after her beloved brother. After returning home with two babies, my dad finally showed up and saw his adorable son and daughter.

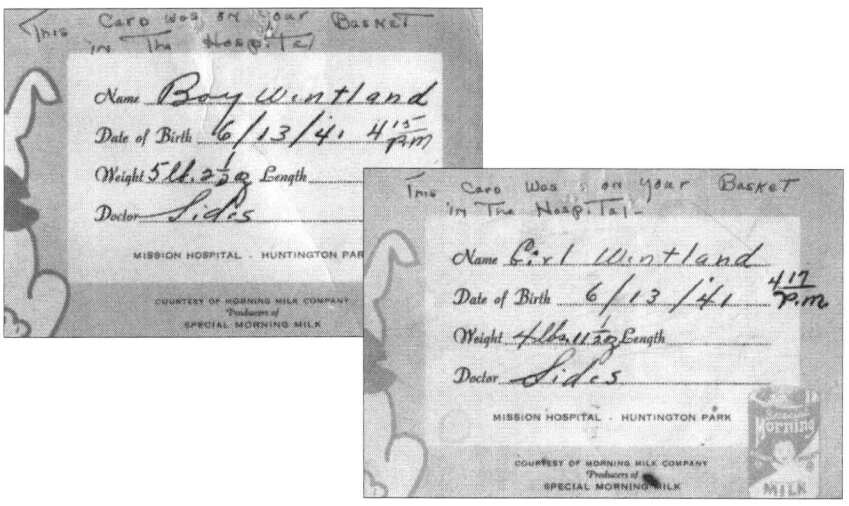

61

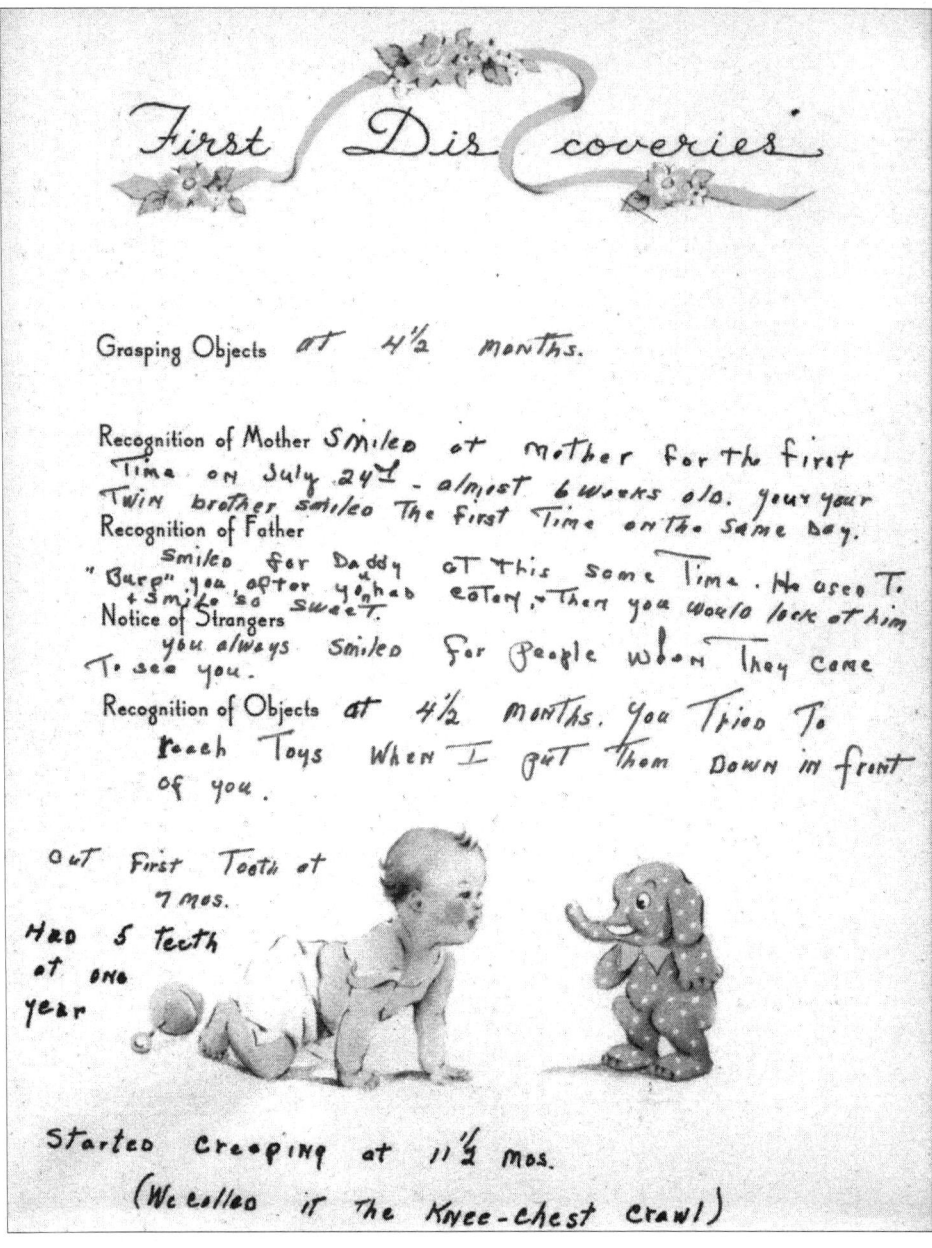

Page from Jeanie's baby book

My dad read an article in the newspaper telling about a newly-formed group known as Alcoholics Anonymous. He attended meetings and after treatment was able to stop drinking. He found a job tending vending machines, and we children sometimes accompanied him.

On November 7, 1942, they had me, their fourth child. I was born at home as it was during World War II and the hospitals were overfilled with patients. Because my mother had delivered two previous pregnancies in the hospital, she was required to deliver at home with the help of a midwife. I didn't get a birth certificate because I was born at home. All I have is a postcard with my name, my mother's name, and a notice saying "Important – Save for entering school." The Wentland family was now complete with two boys and two girls.

While living in Los Angeles, our close and loving family played together. Our dad built many of our toys, and we often spent our days together going to the beach, on a picnic, or just playing together in our fenced yard. World War II created hardships for everyone, changing the lifestyles of many. Blackouts were common in the evening and food was rationed. My mother told of baking only one birthday cake for the twins on their first and second birthdays because sugar was rationed and in short supply.

In June 1947, several months following our move to Berlin and after several years of no alcohol, one beer rekindled my dad's drinking habit, which continued for several years. He participated in a second treatment session and then remained sober the remainder of his life.

A very strong, loving, and stable man, Harvey was Jeanette's support system. Most people who knew him were not aware of his alcoholism and those who did hear of it found it hard to believe Harvey was once "a drinker." Because of his heart condition and the limited type of work he was able to do, he was, at times, unemployed. My mother used her secretarial skills to become the primary breadwinner.

After appropriate medical care, my dad returned to a full-time job for over twenty years as a salesman. His health began failing again and he began collecting Social Security at age 62. My mother continued work as a secretary and my dad became the house-husband. One habit neither of them could break was smoking cigarettes. They both remained lifetime smokers.

As a young family, together we attended church, went fishing and swimming, rented a cottage on Silver Lake for a week each summer, went for car rides, and walked downtown for ice cream cones. One Saturday afternoon, our mother roller-skated around the block with us kids. Her former priest, whom she hadn't seen in years, surprised us with a visit, and we were delighted that he saw our mother skating with us.

Our dad was an active member of the Masonic Lodge in Berlin. This was a united group of men who donated millions of dollars annually for hospitals; helping widows, orphans, and the aged; relief for people in distress; and scholarships for students. One Christmas Eve, after returning home from church, we found two large boxes on our front porch. Toys and family articles filled the boxes which made our day a happier celebration at a needed time. One of the toys was an organ grinder that Georgie played with. Our parents told us later that the gifts were from the Masons.

My father was my mother's sponsor when she joined the Order of the Eastern Star, a fraternal organization of Master Masons and their wives who perform some of the same duties as the Masons. She was an active member and held an office. For special meetings, we were proud to see her in her long, formal gown and high-heeled shoes, with her red-painted fingernails. She looked so beautiful.

Our parents were not social climbers or club-oriented people. They were active in church, our school activities, and the PTA. They volunteered and helped people in need through their personal lives as well as their Masonic memberships. However, they felt they didn't fit in with most other couples because they weren't alcohol drinkers.

I joined the Job's Daughters at the age of 16 and remained a member until I reached Majority which is age 21. To become a member, I needed a sponsor who was a Mason, as a parent could not sponsor his own child. My father's brother, Clarence, who was a high-ranking Mason, did the honors. This organization inspired respect for parents and a love for home, country, and the Bible. I believe my membership in that group was a positive influence on my morals and lifetime behavior.

The death of the twins and the sickness of another child were devastating to each of us. We faced the tragedy individually, quietly, and sorrowfully, with a hurt so deep that we were not able to talk about it. One day, my mother explained to Jack and me that it was not uncommon for couples to divorce after losing a child. She added that parents would sometimes blame each other for the death. Jack and I were told that a divorce would never happen between her and our dad, that no one was to blame for our family's misfortune. We then talked about helping a family each year at Christmas time in memory of Jeanie and Georgie. We all agreed to help a family with children. My parents continued this practice until their deaths.

During the year before his death, my dad told me that he and my mother discussed their life together. He shared that, along with the bad, they were blessed with love for each other along with many good times. I feel they counted their blessings and honored "The Pledge" they made on September 10, 1938.

# FROM SUNNY CALIFORNIA TO SNOWY WISCONSIN

During the early family years, we lived in sunny California: an idyllic life of beaches, palm trees, sun, outside play, and, yes, movie stars! We spent our days together in the fenced backyard and often at the Santa Monica Beach. My father fished the ocean while my mother and we children played in the sand and water. Life was fun!

Jeanette and Harvey with their four children:
Left to right: Georgie, Jo on Jeanette's Lap, Jeanie, with Jack
below in front – 1943

67

Dad Harvey with kids            Mom Jeanette with kids

The Wentland Children: Jack, Georgie, Jeanie, and Jo - July 1946

One day our parents announced we would be moving to a state called Wisconsin. Although I was only four years old at the time, I remember hearing we would be driving through a state called Oklahoma and another called Illinois, and the ride in the car would be very long.

Because the trip to Wisconsin would be long and we would be living with our grandparents who had deteriorating health, we would be unable to take Brownie, our dog. The day before we left, we gave Brownie to a family with children. We all said our sad good-byes to our beloved pet.

In March 1947 we closed the door for the last time at our home at 611 West 65th Street in Los Angeles. Our small gray Ford was packed

69

with boxes and suitcases as well as the entire Wentland family: Dad Harvey, Mom Jeanette, and children, Jack age seven, twins Georgie and Jeanie age five, and me, Jo, age four. As we were backing out of the driveway to begin our journey, my father glanced out the rearview mirror and saw Brownie running towards us down 65th Street with his rope leash dragging behind. Four kids in the backseat excitedly opened the door, Brownie jumped in, and we were on our way to Wisconsin.

We were driving through Oklahoma when my mother told us that sometimes the people of Oklahoma are referred to as "Okies," and that was not a nice name. We were warned to not call anyone an "Okie."

We stopped at a gas station, and the four of us kids and Brownie, who sat by and on our feet, piled out of the car to stretch our legs. My mother almost had heart failure when she saw Georgie walk up to the filling station attendant. Once again, she had just gone over the lesson on not using the name "Okie," and she feared what would come out of this 5-year-old's mouth. Georgie, the skinny, freckled-faced, brown-haired kid with beautiful blue eyes, looked up – way up – to the man filling our car's tank and said, "Hi...I like you!" However, my mother did not relax until we were again on the road. Her apprehension is easily understood as Georgie was always where the action was. If an event occurred, he was either the cause or a big part of it. He was a creative and inquisitive boy who attracted, created, and absorbed trouble.

We arrived in Assumption, Illinois, and stayed one night with Uncle

Mert, Aunt Olive, and cousins Francis Jean, John, and Mary Lou. This was our first encounter with snow. We all played outside wearing our cousins' snow pants, boots, mittens, jackets, and hats. What fun we had!

Their house had a large outside door angled near the ground. To open the door took the strength of the two older kids. We were surprised to see a stairway going down and under the house. This was the Wentland kids' first exposure to a basement. Our cousins' house also had a stairway inside that led to second-floor bedrooms, another new experience for us.

Early the next day, our family, including Brownie, got back into the gray 1936 Ford for the final day of our trip to Wisconsin. By this time, all of us were tired and bored. From us kids in the backseat, my parents repeatedly heard, "It's my turn to sit by the window. Brownie, move. There's more snow," and the inevitable, "How many more miles?"

At last, we arrived at my grandparents' home in Berlin. No beaches, palm trees, ocean, or sand. However, we were overjoyed to see plenty of snow, beautiful evergreen trees, and a park across the street. Brownie was excited too.

While Jack and the twins went to Washington School to finish out the year, I sat on the floor in our empty living room to watch out the window for the big moving van that finally delivered our belongings.

Georgie with Brownie – 1947

West Side Park across the street from our grandparents' home.

Jackie, Georgie, Jo, Jeanie – 1947

My grandparents' home was a duplex. We lived in the other side of their home. We had a living room, two bedrooms upstairs, plus an outhouse in the back. Meals were eaten with my grandparents in their kitchen, since we didn't have one.

Grandpa and Grandma Wentland

My grandpa was a cranky person. He believed children should be seen and not heard but after our family moved to Spring Street, one mile across town from my grandparents' home, we three younger kids would sometimes ride our bikes to their house to pick raspberries and other garden items. And we would occasionally stay overnight.

Even with his limited schooling, my grandpa was a head-strong, resourceful, and hardworking man. He created many homemade and

73

ingenious tools to help him complete his chores. He always had an answer for a question asked of him. His thinking was "always give an answer – as a question wouldn't be asked if the person knew the answer!"

In his elderly years, my grandpa used more of his ingenious ways of doing things. On Saturday nights he would bathe and get himself ready for church the next day. He was dressed except for his trousers. Those he laid neatly between the mattress and springs in his bed. His pillows were propped against the headboard of his bed so he could sleep sitting up and not wrinkle his white shirt and tie. In the morning, he removed his pressed trousers from under the mattress, put them on, and he was ready to attend church.

My grandma always had time for children and loved to sit with us. She would visit, cuddle, and ask questions as she rubbed and tickled our hands and arms. One question she loved to ask was "Who is your favorite...grandma or grandpa?" Our answer was always "You, Grandma!" Her Cheshire grin revealed her approval and we would all laugh. Sometimes Georgie, Jeanie, and I would spend the night at my grandparents' house. When we were settled in bed together, we would begin to giggle and ask Grandma if she would remove her false teeth. We'd start laughing before she reached into her mouth to grab her entire set. At that moment, her mouth would cave in and she would walk out of the room. Her teeth would be soaked in a glass of water on her nightstand until she needed them the next morning. Our giggling continued even after she left the room. She was a typical doting, cookie-baking grandma.

My grandparents often played cards with another couple, the Schroeders, who lived nearby. The men had their own opinions and didn't always agree. At times they would argue over the game or their political differences. Their wives sat quietly as the men's voices would rise. Soon the Schroeders would leave the game and go home. After time passed, they would get together for another night of card playing. One thing about which my grandpa was certain: "Ma isn't going to be laid next to Schroeder" in the cemetery. The Schroeders' cemetery plot was next to my grandparents' plot. Grandpa and Mr. Schroeder were laid next to each other with their wives on opposite ends.

After about a year, we moved from my grandparents' home in Berlin when my parents bought a house in Spring Lake, a small unincorporated community 20 miles northwest of Berlin. The cost of the old farmhouse, which had no plumbing, was $2000. A pump was outside near the kitchen door where we kids pumped water for cooking and bathing. The outhouse was a distance from the house itself, near the rubble remains of a barn that had burned years before.

We four kids attended a one-room schoolhouse within walking distance from our house. We walked the dirt road to school and through the sand-burr lot before entering the school building. Jack was in fourth grade, the twins were in second grade, and I was in first grade. The school sat between Fuller's General Store where my dad worked and the local church.

My mother was working at the Berlin Chapman Company and took the bus to and from work each day. We kids enjoyed walking down the dirt road to meet the bus when she came home. The bus driver would give us a ride home with our mom.

One time I had to stay home from school because I was sick. My dad wasn't working, and he was supposed to take care of me but, instead, he took me to a neighbor lady's home. The lady's husband and my dad went out drinking together. I was sad about the choice he made.

Jo and Jeanie in a tub at their home in Spring Lake

Our family lived in Spring Lake about six months when my parents announced we would be moving back to Berlin. I never knew the reason. An older couple bought the house and requested that our dog Brownie be included in the sale. The lady was blind and Brownie would be a help to her. Brownie's most important job was to lead her to the mailbox at the bottom of the long, hilly driveway. We became good friends and were able to visit them occasionally.

One time, the couple, who bought our house in Spring Lake, was going out of town and asked us if we could watch Brownie while they were gone. We didn't tell our dad about the surprise visitor. We were all upstairs when we heard Daddy come home from work. Brownie recognized his voice and he got so excited that we couldn't hold him. He went running down the stairs and the two were happily reunited. That was a happy time for us, especially for Brownie.

We rented a large four-bedroom duplex on a busy highway. The adjoining unit was an apartment occupying a small part of the first floor. When I saw the house at 109 Spring Street, I felt we were rich because the upstairs had a large bathroom with a big bathtub, a toilet, and a sink. We had just moved from a small house where, on a Saturday night, we would bathe in a metal washtub placed on the living room floor next to the stove that heated our whole house.

We were away from the country and in the city again. Other children lived in homes nearby and we soon found friends. Schools were near, the East Side Park was one block away, shops were a short walk, as was the church. We rode our bicycles to Grandpa and Grandma Wentland's house across town to help them with their garden. Settling was easy and life was fun!

Mrs. Hall, a very nice elderly lady, rented a small part of the first floor as her apartment. She endured a lot of noise from us. We had a cigar box full of marbles that we'd empty at the top of the stairway, laughing and squealing as the marbles bounced down each step making a lot of racket. Her apartment wall was at the bottom of our stairs. She either didn't hear us or she didn't mind. We were kids at play while our parents were at work.

When we were small children and my parents were working, we had several different girls who were our caregivers. This was in the early 1950's and not at all common that a mother worked and hired a caregiver for her children. Some lived with us during the week and slept on a cot in Jeanie's and my bedroom. My mother was careful when hiring the person who would be caring for her children, or so she thought.

Vicky was one of the caregivers who worked for us one summer. Several years after her employment with us, she was arrested, convicted, and imprisoned, along with her boyfriend, for murdering her husband. When we read the story in the newspaper, we recognized her name and were entertained by the report.

## A CHRISTMAS REMEMBERED

One of the most exciting childhood days is December 25$^{th}$. Follow me as I journey back to our family Christmas in 1950.

Georgie's Christmas letter to Santa, December 1950, text is as follows:

*Dear Santa and Billy and Larry,*
*I an glad that you are back on the*
*radio. I have been listening all of*

*the time. All i want for chirstmas
is a two wheeler bicycle and a micky-
mouse watch and anything a 9 years-
old boy would like. Don't for get my
siters and brother and my mother and
daddy and grandma and grandpa and
all other boys and girl I injoy your
prowgram.
fron George wentland 109 south spring
street Berlin wisconsin*

We were four anxious children eagerly waiting for Christmas morning. However, three of us were unable to wait. Our large house was quiet when our older brother, Jack, opened the door to my sister's and my bedroom and whispered, "He was here...let's go downstairs!" Jeanie and I excitedly jumped out of bed and followed Jack down the creaky wooden steps. Georgie refused to join us. Even our sibling prodding could not change his mind.

The closer we came to the bottom step, the more excited we became. Jack, our leader, was the first to see the bounty under the Christmas tree as we three crept into the room. A bright red scooter, marked with Georgie's name and silhouetted by the moonlight, caught our attention. Even after Jack's trip back to Georgie's bedroom to quietly report Santa's gift, Georgie did not want to join us in our adventure.

Jeanie and I were overjoyed to see a miniature playhouse that included rooms of furniture. We immediately sat on the floor and began to arrange the rooms while Jack rode Georgie's scooter around our large dining room table. I remember glancing away from the playhouse long enough to see his blonde curly head sailing past the chairs.

Suddenly our parents appeared in the doorway. They too saw the blonde curly head in motion and two little girls busy at play. The joyful atmosphere quickly changed to one of dread as we three were directed back to bed.

Jeanie and I cried as we climbed into our opened bed sheets. We felt sad that we had spoiled the surprise of Christmas morning. Temptation got us; however, Jack didn't appear to be affected by his decision.

When Christmas morning arrived, Georgie excitedly got us out of bed. Jeanie and I were delighted to see a surprise from Santa that we had not noticed in our midnight excursion. My father proudly removed a large canvas cover that concealed a home-built cabinet...just like the one our mother used in the kitchen.

Georgie had a wonderful Christmas morning. The whole family watched his brown wavy head sail past the dining room chairs as he rode his shiny red scooter.

Clockwise from top: Jack, Georgie, Jeanie, Jo

## FAMILY TIES

The year is 1995. Help is now available for families suffering multiple tragedies. We are offered more opportunities and options than ever before. In 1955, these choices did not exist. Support groups were not in existence, a counselor was an "advisor," and only "crazy" people visited a psychiatrist. People spoke only of pleasant events. They kept their sick and disabled loved ones either sheltered at home or placed in institutions. People struggled to make a living and raise their families. Financial or emotional help was not expected nor readily available.

In August 1955, when the polio epidemic spread across the Midwest, it left an indelible mark in Berlin, Wisconsin, as it struck our meager population of 4,500. Several families were affected by the disease that claimed the lives of my 14-year-old twin sister and brother. Within six days, the virus, after taking its toll on our family, sent my older brother Jack to the hospital. We were distraught to think a third victim in our family would succumb to the dreaded disease. However, he, along with others in Berlin who were stricken, survived. And, he, unlike other survivors who were disabled, had minor long-lasting effects.

People within our small town, feeling the devastation of my family, helped with monetary gifts, food, and prayer. However, fear of the disease was pervasive, causing these caring people to avoid contact with my family and our home. No one knew for sure how the disease was carried and a treatment or cure was unknown.

The trauma left me, a 12-year-old fourth child and baby of the family, alone to cope with the loss, confusion, and fear. The Berlin residents, my relatives and classmates, as well as friends of the twins, were truly affected by this horrible tragedy. Sadly, feelings were never shared and the damaging lack of help with the grieving process remained with me and the others.

Because I never took the opportunity to share my story with anyone, I felt compelled to take care of the matter *now*. My tardiness is partially due to the sadness and hurt it would cause me when, after all, I should be enjoying life. However, now, many years later, it is time to heal and reach some closure of how the loss of my twin siblings affected my entire life. I phoned several of my cousins to hear their story, and they, too, were now ready to express the feelings that had been locked up for so long.

Cousin Mike, now living in Alaska, was 15 years old at the time of the deaths. He, his two brothers, and two friends had attended a picnic with my family in Green Lake mere days before Jeanie died. After Georgie died, the gamma globulin serum was delivered to the doctor's office by police transport. All the boys who attended the picnic received the gamma globulin injection. They were all petrified of the disease, and it was imperative that they receive the injection and not be allowed to

85

attend the funerals. Mike told of fainting after the injection, feeling relief that he "made it" and was automatically protected.

Cousin Judy, only six days older than the twins, shared a special bond with Jeanie. The two looked forward to the one week they spent together each summer at her home in Madison. She remembers being told of Jeanie's death while she was working at Party Port E, the grocery and liquor store her dad managed. She cried as she continued with her job.

Cousin Joyce, one year older than the twins, also shared special times with Jeanie. Their friendship, kept active through the mail, was rarely interrupted. They dreamed of going into the nursing profession together. Joyce went on to fulfill her dream without her cousin. She saved the last letter she had written to Jeanie the day before Jeanie died. Never mailed, the letter remained sealed and stored in her Bible.

Two days after my telephone call to Joyce, I received a letter from her. A short note was wrapped around the letter she intended to send 40 years ago, "After our conversation last night, I went to my Bible and got the letter and opened it. You may have it." Perhaps Joyce's healing has begun also.

Woodruff, Wisconsin
August 20, 1955

Dear Jeane,

I am sorry to hear you have strept throat. We have all had colds here too. I had a cold and a cough for over six weeks.

I finnaly got my typewriter. It is a Smith-Corona Sterling. It is a portable with everything an office machine has. It cost over one-hundred dollars but the dealer gave me quite a large discount.

I can't wait for school to start. I have most of my school supplies ready, because I have to work right up to Labor Day. I am taking up algebra, English, biology, home eocnomics, typing, band, and some form of vocal work. I don't know if I'll take forensics or not. I hope I can get out physical education so I will have a study hall or two.

I have some schoolclothes I will send down one of these days. I hope they fit.

Last night it it rained. It is a little cooler out now than it was yesterday but it is slowly warming up again.

We have been canning peaches, beans ect. here. I received two first prizes at the fair this year, they amounted to about two dollars. On one one ride I got in for under twelve years of age. The kid with me was sixteen and he got in for under twelve too.

Please excuse some of my spelling and spacing. Write soon.


Love,

Joyce Wentland

87

```
Joyce Wentland
Woodruff,Wisconsin


                    Miss Jeanette Wentland
                    I09 South Spring Street
                    Berlin
                    Wisconsin
```

Cousin Keith from Los Angeles wrote me a letter stating that in August of 1955, following his cousins' deaths, he attended a high school Christian Endeavor Camp, a week-long conference that included "lots of good solid teaching." "It really hit me hard," he wrote. "That camp experience combined with my loss showed me how fragile life is, how short it could be, and how much we are not in control. I never was upset with God, but knew He was ultimately in control. Because of that week, I had an overwhelming desire to serve the Lord and not myself." He added, "I would say all the remainder of my life has gone back to that week, as a point of reference." Keith was nearing his 17th birthday at that time.

Another cousin, Tom, who now lives in Austin, Texas, recently expressed his feelings at a family gathering. He said he "felt sorry" because our family had suffered with so much tragedy in 1955, and more, as the years passed. He felt guilty as his life was blessed with good health and good experiences.

Surprisingly, to me, we all dealt with this tragedy in the same manner. We suffered alone and silently, not necessarily by choice, but by standards set by society, family culture, fear, disbelief, guilt, and confusion. It was our introduction to death at a young age – one we were not at all expected to face. The silence, thank goodness, has been broken and I feel I'm being released from the inside out.

Jack, Cousin Keith, Georgie,
at Grandpa & Grandma Wentland's house in Berlin - 1947
Chicken coop in the background

*Jo Ann Wentland Koch*

# THE MURAL

Numerous thoughts were racing through my mind as I climbed the old wooden steps leading to the front door of the house at 109 Spring Street in Berlin, Wisconsin. For many years, I intended to visit our former family home someday to see "It." I finally did in 1995.

My cousin John, who was vacationing from California, accompanied me. As we walked the streets of Berlin, reminiscing about his childhood visits, we gathered the courage to stop at the house my family called home nearly 40 years prior.

We knocked at the door, introduced ourselves, explained our mission, and were welcomed in by Mrs. Behm, the homeowner. She led us through the house which, even after extensive remodeling, still looked like home to me.

We climbed the stairs to the second floor. In the small room straight ahead, Mrs. Behm stood proudly with her arm extended toward the wall directly across from us. "It" was a beautiful painting of a clipper ship sailing through the stormy green sea. The mural measured approximately five feet by seven feet and covered three-quarters of the wall.

Mrs. Behm explained, "After our discovery of this mural, we knew it would remain in our home as long as we did. It is still in its original form.

90

We did nothing to preserve it. The shiny paint is original. When I painted the room, I was careful to keep my brush from touching the clouds, as I didn't want to disturb the artist's impression." She smiled as she added that her youngest son chose that room because of the mural. Both John and I noticed that The Mural was the focal point of the décor.

John and I examined The Mural closely. As we ran our fingers across the masterpiece, we noticed a faint crack crossing one of the many sails. Disappearing in the water's edge, it revealed proof of the aging wall. Mrs. Behm said she felt the colors never faded because it was painted on the west wall, away from the sun.

We were thankful for her permission to take pictures. After viewing the remainder of the house and sharing a visit, we left 109 Spring Street excited and grateful. We had accomplished our mission.

The cause of my anxious anticipation was that it had been 40 years since I had seen The Mural. "It" was not unlike those painted by the old masters, finding recognition after their deaths. In this case, the artist was my brother Georgie. He was an active 11-year-old artist who died three years after completing this masterpiece.

I remembered him carrying a ladder up the stairs, directly into his bedroom. He had found remnants of paint in the basement, and bringing them up to his "canvas" required several more trips up the stairs. He had found a picture of a clipper ship that spurred his artistic creativity and motivation. While watching him scurry around the house, the rest of the family wondered *now* what is Georgie up to!

I remember him sketching pictures whenever he held a pencil, crayon, or even a stone found in the driveway. He was content with anything that would leave a mark, and he truly loved to draw...anything anywhere. The remains of his artwork found scattered throughout our home were discarded each week on cleaning day. Thankfully, this one piece was not destroyed.

NOTE: As of this writing, the house at 109 Spring Street was sold. The new owner, at the request of Mrs. Behm, was asked to allow The Mural to remain. Unfortunately, when Spring Street, also known as Highway 49, was rebuilt, the cherished old wall in Georgie's bedroom was damaged by the vibration of heavy equipment used to build the road. The new owners were unable to save the painting.

# FAMILY LIFE

# THE FAMILY TREE

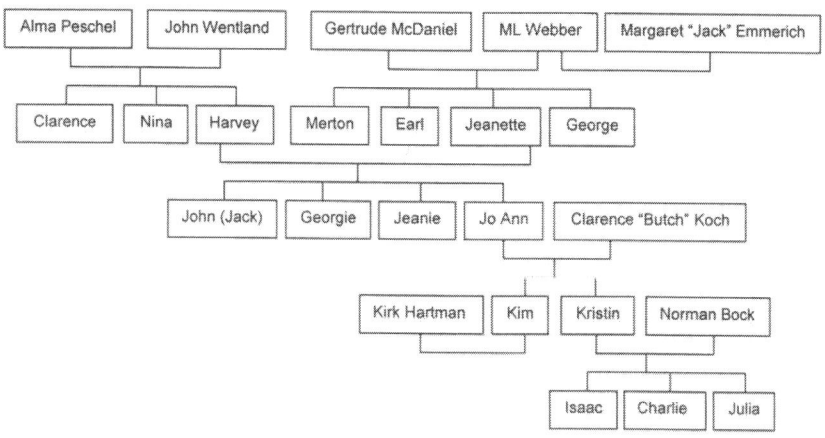

## MY FAMILY

### Jeanie

My sister Jeanie was a clone of our mother. Slightly more than 1½ years older than I, she was my model. Having the same build and features, we were often mistaken as the twins. I sometimes was a "tag-along" as she played with her friends. We shared a bedroom, a bed, household chores, babysitting jobs, clothes, secrets, and stories. The stories were shared after we were to be quiet in our bed at night. We giggled a lot!

Jeanie and I liked playing together with our dolls. One day while we were in Schultz's Dime Store, we discovered a doll we both immediately fell in love with. Often we visited the store just to look at and hold the doll. Deciding to put our own earned and saved money together, we bought the doll we both loved so much. After discussing names for our new doll, we agreed to call her Nancy Jean. Nancy Jean had a cloth body with soft rubber arms, legs, and head. One hand was squeezed closed with a thumb that would fit into her mouth. She had a crying face that looked real; in fact, Nancy Jean was real to us. We didn't disagree about whose turn it was to hold her or play with her; she was always "our" doll.

One day as we were playing "house" on our front porch with several friends, Jeanie, in our play, was going to run away. She carried a long stick with her clothes tied on the end in the classic "hobo" style. I was "so into" our acting that I began to cry, believing my sister was going to leave our family. One of our playmates comforted me by reminding me we were just playing and Jeanie was not really going to leave.

Jeanie, neighbor Carol, Jo in the early 50's

Our father, mother, and brothers loved to fish. Sometimes after supper, we would all pile into the car and drive to my father's favorite fishing spot in Auroraville, a small village seven miles from our house. As the rest of the family fished, Jeanie and I would sit together and braid wildflowers we found near the fishing pond. We'd connect our long braided flowers together and hang the strand across the top of our painted metal bed when we returned home.

At times we would stick our chewing gum on the bedpost when we went to bed at night, and in the morning, we'd pick the wad off the bedpost and chew it again. Little pieces of paint were mixed into our gum but that didn't matter to us.

At one time Jeanie was interested in movie stars. She would cut out pictures of her favorites from magazines and tape them to the walls on her side of our room. The walls on my side remained unchanged showing the large flowered wallpaper that had been there for years before we moved into that house.

We enjoyed singing together, harmonizing songs from a church hymnal or playing our clarinets. When we were not using the music stand to hold our music, we would remove the top and use the lower part as a microphone. Walking around the bedroom telling jokes and singing was silly and fun.

Jeanie and some friends were exchanging thoughts and ideas one day, not long before school was to start. She remarked that nothing ever happened in the small town of Berlin. Not long after the conversation, she was the first person in Berlin to contract and die of polio. Then there was Georgie's death and Jack's hospitalization. And eight months later, our small town was hit by a tornado that destroyed many homes and took the lives of eight people. These were the most devastating news articles in the history of Berlin in many years.

Jeanie's favorite song was "Autumn Leaves." She enjoyed hearing it on *The Lawrence Welk Show* on television the night before she died. I still cannot bear to hear that song.

Georgie, Jeanie and Jo with their clarinets - 1955

### Georgie

Georgie, a clone of our father, was a boy filled with activity, ambition, and excitement. I would often play with him and his friends. Georgie was a left-handed artist and could quickly draw a picture on demand. A real heart warmer, he had brown wavy hair and beautiful blue eyes accented by long, curly eyelashes. His face was peppered with freckles. We three – Georgie, Jeanie, and I – were similar in size at one time, appearing as triplets.

I remember playing with Georgie the day he found some matches. I was three years old and he was four. We were playing in our garage when he lit a match and started a fire. Before long, we heard sirens and saw the approaching fire truck. I was afraid so I ran into the house and hid behind my parents' opened bedroom door. Georgie remained outside and watched the firemen. After the fire was extinguished, the fireman talked to him. They then went into the house and found me in my safe hiding place. We were both scolded.

One time, my mom and dad kissed in front of us and Georgie said, "I think Mommy and Daddy are getting "marreet." My parents didn't display their affection for each other very often. My mother said that she and my dad never told each other they loved each other. She'd continue, "We just knew."

Life was fun and exciting for my 9-year-old inquisitive brother Georgie. He had a curious love for birds and squirrels as they gathered for food at our back door. One day he decided to invite his favorite squirrel "Fluffy" into our house. From a wall outside, not far from the porch leading into the kitchen, I quietly watched Georgie take two walnuts, one in each hand. He began hitting them together and simultaneously clicking with his mouth as he backed into the kitchen door with Fluffy following. They were well on their way into the dining room when our dad appeared. When Daddy realized what was happening and could foresee the potential havoc the squirrel could cause, he calmly said to Georgie, "Now slowly move toward the door as you keep hitting the nuts together." Georgie obeyed as he led Fluffy back out the door. I don't remember what happened after Fluffy was outside again, but I do remember hearing the damage that a wild animal such as a squirrel could cause inside a house.

Georgie and Jeanie, Spring Lake – 1948

Our father and a cousin built a fishing boat that Daddy named the "Fanny Buster." He and Georgie went fishing one afternoon, and as they were waiting for a fish to bite, Georgie said, "I decided to quit smoking." He said he wanted to play sports and knew he couldn't be a smoker if he did. Georgie was 11 years old at the time. Our dad told me the story several times and we always had a good laugh.

Georgie in boat, announcing he was going to quit smoking

In Berlin, riding double on a bicycle was against the law. One day, Georgie and I were riding double on his bicycle and the Chief of Police, Gerry Beck, saw us. He asked me to get off the bicycle and walk home. Gerry, who was a friend of our family, discussed the issue with my mother, and they decided we were to write "I will not ride double" on a sheet of paper, 100 times. We were about eight or nine years old at the time. I remember taking my completed assignment to the police station promising I would never ride double again. Soon after, my parents bought me my own used bicycle.

When our father worked at the Gamble store in Berlin, Friday night was the one night of the week the stores were open. That was the time many families did their weekly banking and shopping. If my father had a "good week" selling televisions or appliances, he would bring home a half-gallon of ice cream for our family. We looked forward to this treat. If he returned home without ice cream, we knew it was not a good week. Everyone was disappointed except Georgie. He wouldn't say anything as he went into the kitchen, but soon we would smell and hear popcorn being made for everyone. Georgie always had a positive attitude and a smile.

I recently talked with Donna, a girlfriend of Georgie's the summer he died. He painted her name on the back fender of his bicycle. Donna said he gave her a kiss. How sweet to hear that!

Our mother always cooked healthy and delicious meals for our family. Vegetables were important; however, peas were not a favorite, especially to Georgie and me. We had to sit at the table until everything on our plate was eaten. I remember filling my mouth with peas, going outside on our front porch and spitting the peas between the cracks on the steps, down to the ground. After the twins died and we moved to a smaller house, my mother found dried-up peas under the table leaf where Georgie sat. She said they were lined up like little soldiers. We had to smile.

Georgie, Jeanie, and I had our tonsils out together at the hospital in Berlin. I was six years old and in a crib. The twins were seven and in single beds. I remember standing up and looking at them. We didn't talk because our throats were sore.

Georgie, Jeanie, and I were not baptized as babies, as our brother Jack, and needed to have that blessing before confirmation in the Methodist church. Before the service for confirmation began, the three of us were baptized. The twins were confirmed that same day and I was ready for confirmation the next year. When they died, I felt satisfied we three were finally baptized.

The three of us seemed to be together nearly all the time; either I was with Georgie while Jeanie was with her friends, or I was with Jeanie when Georgie was with his friends. Jack was a couple years older so he wasn't interested in our activities.

Georgie and Jeanie, Baptism and Confirmation,
Berlin Methodist Church

## Jack

Jack hung out with his friends. He was older and his interests were different from his three younger siblings. He was born with beautiful golden curls and always took pride in his appearance. A moody boy, being a very opinionated person made it difficult to see Jack's warm, kind side.

Jack was artistic like our father and Georgie. He oil-painted scenes of his favorite fishing and hunting areas. He and Georgie had shared a

105

bedroom but to have more privacy, he moved to a large storage room where he could be by himself. The three of us were not allowed in his room. One day, we sneaked into his room and discovered the pencil drawings of several Esquire girls. Of course, we teased him. It was not long before he devised a way of knowing if his room was entered. He connected a piece of thread and two tacks across the inside of his door. If the thread was broken or altered in any way, he knew one of us had crossed his threshold.

Jack and his friends were curious, rebellious, mischievous, and sometimes destructive. Jack and his closest friend Gene would ride their bicycles to Auroraville many times to go fishing or flirt with the girls. It was a 15-mile round trip and they would be gone all day. My parents questioned those bicycle trips and were apprehensive about what the two were getting into but trusted they would behave.

One day, he and some friends decided to shoot their BB guns at the big glass windows of the Standard Oil Gas Station across the street from us. It wasn't long before the police were at our house asking for the gun. Jeanie answered the door and had to give the gun to the police. She cried when they left because she didn't want to disappoint her brother. He and his friends had to pay a fine and replace the damaged window.

Jack was beginning his junior year in Berlin High School when he was the third one in our family diagnosed with polio. Jack is thought to have survived polio because the medical staff anticipated the illness and commenced the necessary treatments early.

Jack celebrated his 16th birthday during his two months in the polio ward. An article about him celebrating his 16th birthday in the hospital was published in the newspaper, encouraging readers to send cards.

## Letters From Pals Aid John Wentland In Fight For Health

Friends have been informed that John Wentland, 16-year-old son of Mr. and Mrs. Harvey Wentland, of Berlin, is slowly improving in his fight against polio, the disease which claimed the lives of his twin brother and sister in the last two weeks.

Postcards written for John by his mother inform friends that his temperature is slowly dropping each day, but that he is still "a sick boy". But his mother adds that he's doing "a good job of keeping his chin up".

He is unable to write as long as he is in isolation (at Wisconsin General Hospital, Madison), but he enjoys getting letters from his friends, as they help pass the long hours in bed and it helps to know that he is being remembered back home.

John's parents are staying in Madison at present, and are with him as much as possible. In one message, Mrs. Wentland said, "We are sure he will be OK now but it will be a long time before he will be back to normal. Tell all of the kids to say a prayer. He knows it helps."

His address is:
Wisconsin General Hospital
Orthopedic Clinic
Madison, Wis.

## John Wentland Observes Birthday

Friends of John Wentland were reminded this week that he will celebrate his 16th birthday Thursday, Sept. 8. That is, he will celebrate as much as possible in his bed at Wisconsin General Hospital.

His parents, Mr. and Mrs. Harvey Wentland reported this week that he has been taken out of the isolation ward, and is on the road to recovery. John is suffering from polio, the disease which claimed the lives of his twin brother and sister in August.

Judie, Jack's girlfriend, remembers "how caring Johnny was from the day we met when we were in third grade." She had a toad named Oscar that needed food and Jack helped her find worms in the park for Oscar. Judie and Jack became friends that day and grew to be sweethearts for several years. After returning home from the hospital, he told Judie he didn't want to have children of his own because he didn't want to see them suffer.

His close friend, Gene, said to me in a recent phone conversation, "Jack's personality changed after his bout with polio. He became self-centered and life was all about himself." Gene and Jack had a close, long friendship so I'm sure Jack shared things with Gene that he didn't share with anyone else.

Jack came home in the beginning of November. He continued therapy sessions at Mercy Hospital in Oshkosh and attended his first months of school through a television system connected between our house and his classroom. Finally, he was able to attend high school.

On my 13th birthday in early November, Jack was eager to lead me to my room after I returned home from school. On my bed sat a large, brown, teddy bear with a huge, yellow bow tied around his neck. My new sleeping companion was a gift from my parents. That was the first time in over two months that Jack showed happiness and excitement. I was grateful to see my brother smiling again.

After losing our sister and brother, Jack would jokingly say I was his favorite sister. I would respond by saying he was my favorite brother.

When Jack was in high school, he met several men who were interested in ham radio. We had an uncle who was into that hobby and he taught Jack. He spent many hours talking with and meeting other ham radio operators.

When the tornado devastated Berlin in April 1956, nine months after the polio epidemic, it caused death, devastation, and loss of homes. Jack immediately used his talent as a ham radio operator to help locate friends and relatives of the injured.

My father had just taken Jack to Berlin High School after returning from therapy in Oshkosh when the tornado headed up a hill toward the school. The students gathered at the window and watched in terror as debris swirled. The black clouds hovered over the school as the funnel traveled southeast of the school and over Oakwood Cemetery, destroying the water tower. Jack witnessed the twister picking up an elderly lady he knew, twisting her like a rope and throwing her into the flying rubbish. He slept with lights lit for a long time. This was one story he shared.

As Jack and his friends grew older, they were able to drive cars. Jack was very possessive of any car he had. I was allowed to ride in his car only in an emergency. If he was going to be passing a young girl walking on the sidewalk, I had to slide down off the seat onto the floor so as not to be seen.

Jack's high school photo
at age 16 - 1955

One sunny afternoon Jack invited his friends to our house to wash their cars. As I walked home from a friend's house, I noticed them in the front yard. Lots of talk and laughing was going on when I saw that each boy was using a large white Kotex pad to polish their cars. I was angry, but even more embarrassed that he had gone into my closet and helped himself to my private, girl products.

Jack answered the doorbell one day when I was not home. A boy he disliked asked if I was home. He told the boy to get off our porch and if he ever came back he would throw him off. My parents and I often laughed about that encounter. I was impressed that he cared that much about his little sister and would stand up for me as he did.

After Jack's formal therapy ended, he continued to work out with weights to strengthen his body. However, one arm became smaller and weaker than the other. At times, he'd lose grip on a gallon of milk and the jug would fall to the floor. His legs were also thin. He tried to enlist in the service but was rejected due to having polio and the ensuing complications.

Jack's high school graduation photo - 1957

Although he was a rebel and barely graduated from high school, he began his college education at the age of 21 in the School of Nursing. He and another male were the first two men to attend the University of Wisconsin-Madison as male nurses. Jack later changed his direction and became a successful veterinarian.

My brother Jack introduced me to my husband Butch who lived in Omro, a small town northeast of Berlin. Jack would go hunting with Butch and his brother John. I was heartbroken from a break-up with my boyfriend when Jack said that I should meet John's brother Butch. I was 15, Butch was 16. We dated off and on for seven years before getting married. Butch had a positive attitude and was always in a good mood. We'd laugh and have so much fun. I'd often thank my brother for introducing us and he would brush it off.

**My Mother Jeanette**

My mother Jeanette was a remarkable woman. Attractive, but definitely not a fashionable dresser, her appearance was pleasant and her smile frequent. Born with a head full of natural curls, she was the envy of most women. While we were growing up, my mother was the primary breadwinner. This required the hiring of a housekeeper/childcare provider half a century before it became the way of family life. She often bragged about having four children in 38 months. Her personality, much like Jack's, incorporated unpredictable mood swings, a need to yell or pout, or get away to smoke a cigarette. In spite of these unpleasant traits, she did have a great sense of humor. Ironically, after her high school graduation, she was in the nursing program at the University of Wisconsin in Madison. Finding that not to her liking, she then attended secretarial school. My mother was an independent woman and always said she didn't want to be a burden.

My mother corresponded with a lady in Milwaukee whose name was Mrs. Buretta. She had also lost her first daughter to polio and she had a younger daughter. I felt that Jeanie was my mom's favorite as, at that time, they were close. I felt that Mrs. Buretta and my mother lost their favorite daughters and each had only one left with me as my mother's second choice. I often wished I had died instead of Jeanie and Georgie. I would have traded myself for the twins. Then they would have three kids instead of only two.

I was lonely after losing my twin siblings and asked my parents if we could have more kids in our family. My mother had had a hysterectomy years earlier, and we wouldn't qualify for adoption due to our family finances. My thought (very seriously) was that I could have a baby. I would perhaps miss a year of school, but because I was one of the younger children in my class, I would return the next school year to the class of kids who were my age. It seemed simple and the only solution to my loneliness.

My sincere plan – from the naïve mind of a 12-year-old – was to use my father as the father of the child. We would go into the bathroom (that was the only place where I took my pants down) and "do whatever it was." I would immediately be pregnant and our family would grow. When I told my mother the solution to my dilemma, she gave me a look of disgust, mumbled a word or two, turned around, and walked away. After time passed, I was able to laugh at my misperception as well as my mother's response, but never at my sincerity.


## My Father Harvey

My father Harvey was a most special person to me. A nicely built, handsome man, he was kind and affectionate. His beautiful blue eyes reflected his mild manner. At the young age of 32, he had his first heart attack. On the day he was to return to work at Standard Oil Company in Los Angeles, he had his second heart attack. The company would not rehire him due to his health issues. This disability affected his choice of employment for his remaining working years. A recovered alcoholic for the last half of his 65 years was a true testimony to me, demonstrating his strong will and faith. He was a tenth-grade-educated man and did well in the advertising and sales business in spite of his lack of a high-school diploma.

When we lived in Berlin, we occasionally lived "on the county." My dad had to repay the county when he found work. One time, when we were walking together, he explained it to me, adding, "That's the way it should be. You get help when you need it but then you need to pay it back."

My dad's interests included building toys for his children, photography and developing his photographs, drawing, hunting, and fishing. In his later years, he designed and built a pontoon houseboat he called "The Ship." He and my mother often used it for fishing or just cruising the Fox River. The two cots inside were handy for resting and the portable potty was an important feature for day trips.

Mom Jeanette, Dad Harvey, Jack - 1956
Our first vacation after the loss of the twins
Photo taken by Jo

After August 1955, our warm and loving family became quiet and never regained the closeness we'd previously enjoyed. Even after more than 57 years, the tragic loss remains with me.

## HARVEY'S BABY

When introducing our family, my mother's words, after announcing my three older siblings' names, were "and this is the baby, Harvey's Baby." That title stayed with me, and I was always my dad's baby.

My parents married in 1938. One year later, their first child was born. The twins followed 21 months after that, and, at that time, my parents felt their family of two boys and one girl was complete. These children kept the family busy day and night, not to mention the number of diapers and soakers they used. The year was 1941 and there were no disposable diapers or liners; nor were there plastic pants to cover the cotton diapers that required daily rinsing, washing, line-drying, and folding.

My busy mother told my dad, "If we have any more children, *you* are having them." Seventeen months after the twins were born, my father had me, a second daughter. He gave me the name Jo with the middle name Ann and, in later years, often called me Joey. I was close to him and enjoyed sharing the story of being my dad's baby.

My father passed away at the age of 65 in December 1976. Our family cemetery plot is in a beautiful, gated area, resting on a steep hill that overlooks the east side of Berlin.

Entering through the open gates and continuing up the hill, the road parts east and west, leading to graves from as early as in the mid-1800s. At the split in the road, sits the beautiful Griffiths Memorial Chapel, a gift of a prominent Berlin businessman. It was built in 1923 and includes an entrance arch and gates to the cemetery. At the time of my father's death, the chapel was used to hold bodies of the deceased during the winter. The cemetery's board did not allow gravesites to be opened after November 1. Following April 1, when the ground thawed, the cemetery crew would gather to open the graves for the burial of the deceased stored in the quaint chapel.

The day of my father's funeral, my mother and I discussed spending time together at his gravesite for his burial. The funeral director would notify my mother of the date and time.

One day in early April, as my husband was at work and our two daughters at school, I felt a passion to read, again, the cards and letters I had received when my dear dad passed. At noon, I sat in our recliner, read the many cards and notes, and wept. An hour later, I ate lunch and continued my day. When my husband returned home from work later that day, I told him about "my time with my dad" and how refreshed I felt.

That evening, my mother phoned. She explained she didn't want me to be upset about my dad being buried. She continued, "Your father was buried at noon today." She had attended the short internment along with the undertaker. I was surprised but not upset about the changed intention as I believe the time that I, Harvey's baby, spent remembering my father that afternoon, was more spiritually meaningful than if I had been in attendance at his burial. I felt it was a special time my dad and I were spending together. I was at peace.

My father was buried next to the twins. Two years later, they were joined by my older brother, Jack. My mother passed away 22 years later when she, too, joined them. I remember telling my mother at a time when we were visiting the graves, that one day our family would be together in Oakwood. She remarked, "That's one way of looking at it." My Wentland grandparents are also in our plot and three spaces remain for my husband and me.

Georgie, Jeanie, and I, along with the Walker kids, Diana and Jeffrey, often played in that beautiful cemetery. We walked the grounds as we found it fascinating to read the old names and dates engraved on the historical gravestones. We ate our packed lunches after we climbed on the rugged rock formations in the nearby quarry. I'm sure our parents never knew the whole story about the dangerous excursions we took. Ironically the place we played in the cemetery is very near the location of our family graves.

From left: Jeffrey & Diana Walker, Georgie, Jo, Jeanie – 1950s

*One day while playing together at the Walker's home, we decided to dress up in the old-fashioned apparel stored in their attic. Because we felt we looked so charming, we decided to take a stroll through downtown Berlin. We were approaching the Berlin Journal building when Mr. Don Zahalka, the city editor, asked permission to take our picture. This picture was published in the Berlin Journal at various times over the years. Mr. Zahalka left the Berlin Journal, moved to Oshkosh, and became employed at the Teachers College where he used the photo as an educational tool for many years. Upon his retirement, he gifted the original photo to me. A copy is displayed in the former Walker home which is now the Beckwith House Bed & Breakfast at 179 E. Huron Street.*

## MY FATHER'S FAMILY

My father, Harvey Edward Wentland, the youngest of three children, was born and raised on a farm in the small community of Coloma, Wisconsin. The farm consisted of 100 acres in the southwest corner of Waushara County in central Wisconsin. Harvey was a loving, caring, and thoughtful person from the day he was born. This handsome man was loved by all who knew him.

Harvey's father, John Julius Wentland, married Alma Peschel in 1904. At the turn of the century, John built his first house on the wooded farmland. Their log home contained one big room and a loft. Log stairs resting on the dirt floor led the way up to the loft where the children would sleep.

John Julius and Alma Wentland - 1904

John Julius, my grandfather of German decent, was a hard-working, stern man. He had very little education and could not read or write. He communicated by drawing pictures, and for his signature, he printed the letter X. Despite his lack of education with attending school for only about six weeks, he accomplished many things that were clever, inventive, and well done. His house and property provided evidence of his many ingenious inventions.

The newlyweds spent their days working the land with a horse and plow and caring for their cows, chickens, and garden.

Alma and John Wentland with their two children, Nina and Clarence,
in front of their log home - approx. 1914

*Jo Ann Wentland Koch*

Alma was a sweet and quiet young woman whose religious faith was of great importance in her life. She attended grade school and learned to read and write. After the birth of two children, Clarence and Nina, John felt their family was complete. When Alma announced she was carrying another child, John said it was not his and told her she must have been with another man.

My father, Harvey, was born November 14, 1911. He and his mother were very close, and it was said he was her favorite child. They both had beautiful blue eyes, identical temperament, and were compassionate, trusting, and sincere.

Their three children were born in the log house. As they grew older, John and Alma built a second home that was larger and included a barn and sheds. The old log house was then used for storing firewood and as a stable.

In their home, on Saturdays only German was to be spoken. Harvey refused and remained silent on Saturdays.

The Wentland Family's new home – 1918

Left to right, bottom photo: Alma, Nina, John, Harvey, Clarence

Clarence and Nina completed high school and college to become teachers. Both began their careers teaching in a one-room school. Clarence later became a principal and then went on to become the State Supervisor of School District Reorganization and Consolidation of Wisconsin. He also authored several books on teaching.

Left to right: Harvey, age 5; Nina and Clarence - 1919

Harvey was not offered help in education and finished only his second year of high school. He wanted to become a pastor and would spend time in the woods preaching to the trees though his big brother and sister made fun of him pretending to be a minister. He helped his father on the hilly farm and worked at a filling station in Coloma. Sometimes Harvey and his dad would take the horses into town to visit the tavern. Pulling the wagon home with my grandfather and dad lying in the back, the horses would get them home safely after a night of drinking.

Grandpa Wentland and his horses

Harvey also was a driver for business people who wanted to go to Chicago. He later joked as he wondered if his job was illegal work for the Mafia, which could have been true. After bouts with pneumonia and lung

125

disease that involved the removal of one lung, he drove to Los Angeles to live with his sister, Nina.

Alma was honest and thoughtful with one exception. When my grandfather didn't talk kindly to her, she refused to read mail from their daughter, Nina, who had moved to California. She would make him wait for several days until she felt ready to share the letter. Nina was her father's special girl and my grandmother knew how she could get revenge. She could control my grandfather's behavior when she felt it necessary.

Alma, my grandmother, enjoyed baking cookies and pies. She rarely shared a recipe as she wanted to keep her baking talents "secret." If she decided to divulge the unknown, she would whisper. Her daily apparel was a large necklace, a housedress, apron, thick hose, and cumbersome laced shoes. An attractive woman, Alma was often complimented about her young-appearing, soft facial skin. She was fastidious with her skin care, being careful not to reveal too much of her "secret" remedy.

My grandparents retired from the farm in the 1930s when they auctioned their property and many of their personal possessions. They, too, moved to California to be near their daughter Nina, her husband Howard, and grandson Keith. My grandpa got a job taking care of lawns in Los Angeles and had special names for his customers, such as "Banana Lady," "Woman in the Wilderness," and "The Bird Man." My grandparents returned to Wisconsin in 1946, settling in Berlin, when my grandmother's health was declining. My grandmother's family was predisposed to heart disease and she was often ailing.

John and Alma Wentland on their 50th wedding anniversary in 1954
West Side Park, Berlin, WI

Grandpa Wentland at the Cattle Fair - August 1962

In Los Angeles, Nina became the director of a nursery school known as a model school where visitors learned how to teach. Several days after my 21$^{st}$ birthday, I boarded a train in Oshkosh, Wisconsin, and arrived in Los Angeles three days later. Fulfilling a dream to return to my birthplace, I was greeted lovingly by my uncle Howard and aunt Nina. I lived with them for five wonderful months while my fiancé Butch was in military training.

Each morning my aunt and I taught in her nursery school. In the afternoons, I traveled the state with both my aunt and uncle. I reveled in the royal treatment they showered on me as we explored my birth state 17 years after my family journeyed to Wisconsin.

In 1965, the John Wentland farm was sold to the Pochmann family who restored and used it as a place for weekends and vacations. Ruth Fouts Pochmann named their new property Triple Ridge Farm and wrote a book on the history of the farm. Years later, Nina wrote a postcard to Harvey, stating she remembered that 80 acres of the farm were purchased from Frank White who obtained it in a land grant signed by Abraham Lincoln.

*Jo Ann Wentland Koch*

## MY MOTHER'S FAMILY

My mother, Jeanette Alice Webber, the only daughter of Merton LaMont Webber and Gertrude Garland McDaniel Webber, was born in Chicago, Illinois, on June 27, 1914. Her father was born in 1875 in New London, Wisconsin, and was known as ML.

Standing over 6' 2" tall, ML moved about slowly, quietly, and deliberately. He was a man of a few words – more of a background presence – and was respected by all who knew him. Grandpa ML had a noticeable lump on the back of his neck. We didn't know why it was there or what it was, but we accepted it was just a part of him.

ML graduated from the University of Wisconsin Madison with a degree in engineering and became a successful engineer who traveled with a construction business. The year his youngest child was born, he built a home at 1160 Emerald Street in Madison. The home, to his family, was always known as "1160".

ML smoked a large, fancy pipe and sat in his special, green, wing-backed chair across from the fireplace in his large living room. Here he read the Chicago Tribune newspaper as he listened to the radio and worked the crossword puzzle. At times we kids would be playing games and reading in that room and about us he would remark, "And just to think I started this mess."

130

Grandpa ML and Grandma Jack in their favorite chairs

ML was a boxing fan and enjoyed watching soap operas on television in his later years. In the early evening, ML could be seen putting on his hat and sweater to go for a stroll.

Eating dinner at ML's house was very formal. When you sat down, your hands were washed and you were quiet. Grandpa sat at the head of the table with the food around him, the plates stacked in front of him. He slowly and deliberately carved the meat and served on each plate what he thought you should eat. And you ate it . . . all of it. You had your napkin in a napkin ring and you used it properly. Dinner took quite a while, as you can imagine.

Christmas Eve was a family event at 1160. It included dinner, drinks, and Midnight Mass. His whiskey was hidden in the basement for safekeeping, but it didn't take long for it to be found by the older grandchildren.

ML's generosity was apparent as he was helpful to those in need during World War II and to his family throughout their lifetime. He was fond of opals and would gift beautiful opal rings to the ladies in his family.

When ML visited us in California, he would hold Jeanie and me on his lap and call us "his kittens." We loved his visits. I can't imagine him ever getting angry. He was an old-looking grandpa, very polite and mannerly. My mother remarked that he was always "an old-looking man." He died at the age of 83 and is buried in Madison.

My mother felt her two older brothers, Merton and Earl, were protective of their only sister. Another brother, George, was born two years after my mother. Jeanette and George often played together and remained devoted to each other their entire lives. They were the two children in the family stricken with Infantile Paralysis in the 1920s.

Left to right: George, Jeanette, ML, Grandma Jack, Merton Jr, and Earl

ML married Gertrude Garland McDaniel in 1906. ML was 31 years old and Gertrude was 19 years old. They met on a street car in Chicago. Gertrude left the marriage after 13 years and four children.

After a few years and several housekeepers, ML married Margaret Emmerich. The story I heard is that ML told his four children he would be gone for a few days and would return with a mother for them. According to my mother, "He went up to Wausau, got married, and came back with a mother." His new bride's nickname was "Jack." All of Jack's siblings had nicknames that followed them throughout their lives. The marriage took place in the early 1920s when "Jack" became the mother of ML's four children. It is said that the marriage was one of necessity as ML needed a mother to raise his four children. Jack's nursing career was beneficial almost immediately as my mother Jeanette and her brother George contracted the polio disease. They were about eight and six years old at the time.

Quotes about the frightful experience from my mother's brother George in July 1994: "That was around 1922 when Jeanette and I were taken to the pest house (the City Contagious Hospital on East Washington Avenue in Madison). I remember vividly that an ambulance backed up to 1160 and took us to the pest house. Ya, I can remember the ride and the old ward and wondering where in the hell are we going. We both went." The family believes, because of Jack's nurse's training, she was allowed to care for George and Jeanette in the hospital. We also believe that once she entered the hospital, she was not allowed to leave. She stayed to give care and treatments to her children. George continues, "She (Jack) probably did more for me in insisting I do the exercises and hot towel treatments and massages and all this stuff. It was enough to drive me up the wall – I didn't understand what the hell was going on, but I do now. There would be like one or two hours of treatment in the morning and the afternoon no matter what I wanted to do. We had to do these exercises." She was using the Kenny treatment, and it is said that Jack, as their new mother, taught Jeanette how to do some of the therapy on her brother. My mother in her later life was told if she had children, they would not develop the polio disease. We assumed it meant because she had polio her children would automatically be immune to the disease.

This new mother immediately took control of the family and home, but not without some difficulty. The children had numerous housekeepers who didn't stay very long. My mother once made reference to the fact that they "ran 'em off pretty regularly – that it was kind of a *Sound of Music* deal where the kids would run the housekeepers pretty ragged."

Merton, the oldest child, was often left to discipline his three younger siblings and felt intimidated when he was no longer in charge. His brothers and sister didn't like his authority over them which made for bad feelings. There certainly was a need for a mother at 1160. In time, Jack had the family in order.

ML and his children in front of 1160
Left to right: Merton, ML, Jeanette, George, and Earl
The woman behind Merton is unidentified.

Eventually, 1160 became the gathering place for family. ML's unmarried sister, also named Jeanette Alice, spent her last years living with her brother and Jack. George, Ede, and their three boys lived there while they built a new home. Even with operating the busy home, Jack found time to bake, sew, knit, and crochet items for family. She knit many mittens on strings for her 14 grandchildren. One winter, she made matching winter coats for Jeanie and me. They were our favorite coats as they had big pockets and a wide belt around the waist.

Grandma Jack kept a tidy home with tasteful furnishings. I felt it was proper and formal with everything in place, yet still inviting. Daily, she wore dark-colored, tailored dresses, black thick-heeled shoes, and she always looked respectable. Several children's books and toys, including the ubiquitous pick-up sticks and marble game, were readily available for the young, visiting children. Grandma Jack was not a complainer and generously shared her life with her husband, children, grandchildren, and great grandchildren.

Grandma Jack with the twins,
Jeanie and Georgie - 1941

Grandma Jack with Mom Jeanette – 1941

Grandma Jack and ML – 1948

# I CALLED HIM GRANDPA

I called him "Grandpa" because he was my grandpa. After all, he was while he was married to my Grandma Gertrude. He was her second marriage and his...well, we don't know the number. That didn't matter. What did matter was that he was an amazing man who loved fun and excitement and demonstrated his love and caring nature to my family.

When Bob Matthews and Gertrude divorced, he was still "Grandpa." Their marriage was a union of convenience that allowed them to travel to Europe and perform with a group of circus entertainers to an audience of well-known dignitaries, including Adolf Hitler. Gertrude and Bob traveled extensively with the circus.

Gertrude and Bob with Fran, Jan, and John, Gertrude's grandchildren - 1942

Bob was an entertainer with Ringling Brothers Barnum & Bailey Circus. His act included the presentation of his pet Tuffy, a caged lion. Bob trained Tuffy to snarl at the crack of a lengthy, leather whip.

I had last seen Grandpa when I was four years old and living in Los Angeles. After his and Gertrude's marriage ended and my family moved to Wisconsin, my mother and Bob often exchanged letters and photos. Several years of correspondence passed when we received a photo of the new Mr. and Mrs. Bob Matthews.

When I traveled to California soon after my 21$^{st}$ birthday, Uncle Howard and Aunt Nina fulfilled many of my requests during my visit. One of my most cherished moments was an afternoon spent with Grandpa Matthews and his wife, Liza.

Grandpa and Liza lived in the Alene Apartments on Kenmore Avenue in Los Angeles. Such a Hollywood-sounding address, I thought, but I was surprised when my aunt, uncle, and I found ourselves at the door of an aged hotel.

To get to #306, Grandpa instructed us to use the elevator at the end of the hall. Shortly after we stepped onto the platform, a gate slammed shut and the exposed cables pulled us up to the third floor. As we rode the freight elevator, we watched the cement block walls of each floor pass as it slowly creaked to a stop. Standing only feet away from the gate stood a short, chunky man with a smile that covered his friendly face. "Hi, Grandpa," I said.

"Hi, darling," he responded. "I'd know you anywhere, a picture of your lovely mother."

As he led us to his apartment, he never stopped talking. It was a joyful reunion. Surprisingly, he was dressed as a typical grandfather: long sleeve flannel shirt with amazingly large red-and-black checks, and gabardine slacks held up with Big Mac suspenders. I liked his tennis shoes.

Anxious to see the "home of a star," I followed closely as we stepped into the living room. Tables, boxes, papers, and overstuffed chairs adorned with crocheted doilies circled the medium-sized room. Numerous photos of his circus friends and family decorated the walls and tables. I asked about Liza. "Oh, she isn't well, you know. She's bedridden." At that time, I heard a meek voice calling for Bob, which he promptly answered by leaving the room.

Several minutes passed and then, standing in the bedroom doorway, was a loving elderly couple. Liza was a tiny, fragile, sweet-looking lady, weighing about 80 pounds. Her attire was a bed shirt. Bob announced his "little lady" was ailing, but she wanted to meet us. He proudly remarked, "She was the world's greatest aerialist, you know."

He had sent my family photos of his Liza balancing on a swing, above crowds of people. She wore skimpy apparel that included sequins and a tutu jutting out from her trim waistline. Tiny slippers and a striking head piece completed her outfit.

Grandpa was nursing pneumonia he had developed during the filming of the movie *Roustabout*. He claimed he "got it holding the door closed so the star, that all the girls were crazy over, wouldn't get chilled." He didn't remember the star's name. I excitedly stammered, "Was it Elvis Presley?"

"Yes," he casually responded. At 21, I was madly in love with Elvis, as most girls were in the late 50s and 60s. I am fortunate to have a copy of that movie where Grandpa has a small part acting as a circus barker. *Roustabout* was filmed in 1964 at the time I visited Grandpa and Liza in their home.

Grandpa was no longer entertaining dignitaries with Tuffy, performing for the public, or showing his flea circus at carnivals, and Liza was no longer an aerialist. They were Bob and Liza, a couple who were meant to be together, loving and caring for each other in their elderly years.

At one point in our visit, Grandpa said to me, "I don't know whatever got into your Grandma Gertrude." That statement was followed by silence. I knew he was referring to her leaving her children and no more was said.

Our visit ended with a loving hug and the assurance of keeping in touch. Liza passed away several years after our meeting. Grandpa and I continued corresponding. The last card, a seven-cent postcard dated November 11, 1975, stated he had been released from the hospital, but had to "keep the oxygen handy." Bob and Liza Matthews were buried together in the Forest Lawn Cemetery, Hollywood, California, with their circus family.

Our visit in the spring of 1964 taught me that lives appearing to be glamorous are not always the way they really are. My "Circus Grandpa" had a full life of entertaining and he was a special man to many people. To me, he was exceptional, and I will always call him Grandpa.

143

## GERTRUDE

I liked the name Gertrude. It sounded very elegant to me, and as a young girl, I was impressed by my Grandma Gertrude's dress and style. None of my friends had a grandmother who wore flowing mid-calf dresses that didn't quite conceal the layers of ruffled can-can slips underneath, sheer hose with a straight black seam running up a slender calf, the newest fashion in hats, and red nail polish. A lit cigarette in a stunning holder added to her distinct style. In my young teenager eyes, she was glamorous.

Born Gertrude Garland McDaniel over a century ago, she lived the life that would become more common in the 1990s. As my mother – Gertrude's only daughter – shared stories with my family, I can relate and attempt to understand my mother's negative feelings toward "the woman who never gave me anything but birth."

Gertrude was born in Tennessee, the third of four children. She was referred to as a "beautiful Southern belle" and was spoiled by her two older sisters and younger brother. The entire family enjoyed entertaining and dancing in Vaudeville.

At 19, she became Gertrude McDaniel Webber when she married Merton Lamont Webber, known as ML. I was told they met each other while riding a street car in Chicago. ML was 31 years old and a successful engineer who often traveled with his construction business. He and Gertrude built a beautiful home at 1160 Emerald Street in Madison, Wisconsin, and had 4 children together: Merton, Earl, Jeanette, and George.

Gertrude was not a faithful wife, and in 1919, after several love affairs, she left ML and their children ages 12, 10, 5, and 3 to join family and entertainers in California.

My mother often told this story of the day her mother left: ML was out of town, working on one of his projects, and Gertrude's sister Louise was visiting from California. Gertrude had expressed her unhappiness and desire to leave ML and the children. Louise had traveled to Madison to change her sister's mind. At that time, Gertrude was having an affair with their church choir director, a church scandal. Louise failed in her mission and cried with the children as Gertrude ran out the front door, smiled, and waved goodbye to her family as she got into the backseat of a waiting cab. This would prove to be the most traumatic event in my mother's young life and the lives of her siblings. Merton, the eldest, had to take over as the mom in the family and his siblings all disliked his authority.

Gertrude visited the children when she could afford a bus ticket from California to Wisconsin. Another story often told by my mother was that on one of her visits, Gertrude suggested to ML that she raise the two younger children (my mother and her brother George) and he could raise the two older children (Merton and Earl). ML then threatened to open a sealed letter she had written to one of her lovers while she and ML were still married. This letter, intercepted by the young man's father, was given to ML; however, it was never opened. Her face turned white, she took $500 that ML offered, and she grabbed a candelabra off the mantle as she quickly departed. Her infrequent visits continued until the four children were grown.

Gertrude with her children: Jeanette, age 6, and George age 4, at top;
Merton, age 14, and Earl, age 12, alongside her
at Wisconsin State Capitol in Madison - 1920

ML and Gertrude divorced, and after numerous housekeepers, ML married Margaret Emmerich (nicknamed Jack), who, from that day forward, was called "Mum" by my mother. Ironically, Jack already knew the four children she was later to mother.

Jack, who was a nurse, knew the Webber family several years before her marriage to ML when Gertrude was often hospitalized. Jack described Gertrude as "a fragile lady longing for personal attention." Never having had children, Jack felt it a blessing to raise a "ready-made family." Neither she nor ML ever spoke unkindly of Gertrude; however, ML did remark once that his children's mother was "like a naughty girl." Jack and ML had no children together although Jack is known to have said, "ML wouldn't let me have any babies."

California made Gertrude's life exciting and youthful again, and she dated sailors from a nearby naval base. When I was 21 years old and visited her (she was over the age of 80), pictures of her former sailor friends were proudly on display.

Gertrude's interest in entertaining was rekindled when she met a man whose life offered her that needed excitement. Bob Matthews lived in a travel trailer and entertained with a group of carnival show artists. Gertrude and Bob were "naturals" as entertainers and they traveled extensively with their carnival friends in the United States and Europe.

Gertrude, along with Bob Matthews, acquired an attachment to reptiles, which were used in her act. She displayed snakes coiling their long bodies around her bare arms. She bragged about having a snake in her purse that would appear "suddenly" while dining in a restaurant. When the waitress brought her bill, the snake often allowed her to leave without paying. As the waitress left screaming, Gertrude would pick up the snake, put it back in her purse, and walk out.

Gertrude and Bob had a snake show, a flea circus, and a dancing bears show. Bob had a gift for training animals. When they were traveling together, they collected "critters" found in the desert and stored them in a cigar box for easy access and travel. However, their biggest claim to fame was Bob's performing lion named Tuffy.

Bob acquired Tuffy as a cub and trained him to walk on a tight-wire, sway on an aerial swing, and roar at the snap of Bob's leather whip. As a cub, Tuffy enjoyed licking the salt off Bob's body as they played in the ocean. Tuffy was also one of the roaring lions seen at the beginning of MGM movies.

While in Seattle, my Uncle George, Gertrude's youngest son, watched Bob's act with Tuffy. Between performances, Tuffy was kept in a cage behind the scenes. George told the story: "They got me in – in the cage, and Tuffy was sitting up on a table or whatever, and she (Gertrude) said, 'Just walk over next to him and stand alongside him like you do it every day – don't act frightened or anything – and I'll take your picture.' She was taking the picture on the outside of the cage and I was on the inside. I've just got one picture of me standing next to Tuffy. Right after the camera flashed, Tuffy turned around and looked at me and I got the hell out of there!" George's brothers, Merton and Earl, also had their pictures taken in the cage with Tuffy.

Top: Merton and Earl with Tuffy and Bob
Bottom right: Earl with Tuffy; left: Merton with Tuffy

George with Tuffy

My cousin Mike, George's oldest son, told this story: Bob and Gertrude were traveling with a carnival. He and his parents, George and Ede, went to visit Bob and Gertrude at the carnival. Bob took six-year-old Mike to lunch in a freak tent, and they ate with a bearded lady, the dog-faced boy, the fat man, and the strong man. He added, "I think I sat within a couple of seats of the alligator boy – a real bad case of psoriasis."

After completing secretarial school and moving to California, my mother, Jeanette, met and married my father Harvey. Living only a few miles from the Matthews – and with my parents' admiration of Bob, a new friendship was created. Gertrude and Jeanette became reacquainted. Sadly, Gertrude's behavior proved to be unchanged as my mother told of the time she invited Gertrude for a visit with her and us four children for a day. Gertrude announced, as we were riding in her car, she knew a man she wanted us all to meet: a "handsome young sailor" that we were sure to "love." My mother ordered Gertrude to immediately turn the car around and return us home, adding, "I will never do to my children what you did to yours."

As a young man, Earl, Gertrude's second son, visited his mother to give her a chance of having a relationship with him. What truly transpired remains lost between Earl and Gertrude but he perceived she tried to "pimp" him – his words. That experience ended any friendship that might have been. My cousin, Jan, said that her father Earl refused to ever see his mother again after she attempted to use him as a "pimp." Gertrude did correspond with postcards (written in green ink) sent to his family, and Gertrude did visit Earl's wife and children one day when Earl made sure he was not home. Because of the unfortunate encounter, Earl's four daughters saw Gertrude only once.

When I was a small baby, I spent a night with Gertrude. When my mother arrived to take me home the next morning, she saw me sitting in a basket on a table. Alongside me, in another basket, was a coiled, small boa constrictor snake. Grandma Gertrude stated we were "two of her babies." That was the last of my overnight visits with my grandma Gertrude.

Grandma Gertrude Matthews with grandchildren - 1943
Left to right: Mike Webber, Jo, Tommy Webber, Jackie;
seated: Georgie and Jeanie

These are only two of many occurrences that happened with the uniting of Gertrude and two of the children she never gave "anything but birth."

Gertrude and Bob Matthews divorced after my family moved to Wisconsin, though we continued corresponding with both. We immediately recognized Gertrude's letters by her beautiful handwriting in green ink.

Several years later, one of Gertrude's letters included an announcement of her marriage to William Bell. William, a widower who claimed to be a distant relative of Alexander Graham Bell, was a nice man who cared for Gertrude and her family as well as his own. The new Mr. and Mrs. William Bell occasionally traveled by bus across the U.S. to visit their children. They were welcome in our home.

In 1964, while I vacationed in California and visited the Bells, I found they resided in two trailers that were side by side. William had a tidy home where he prepared and served their meals. Gertrude's trailer revealed cluttered tables of aged shoe boxes containing numerous dated pictures of sailors in uniform and herself. It was evident to me that she spent her days reliving the past.

I was delighted to see pictures of her 14 grandchildren along the windowsills even though she couldn't recite our names. I recall her looking at my high school graduation picture uttering she didn't "know who that one is." She did recognize the twins who had died nine years previous and commented how sad that was.

The accumulation of the aged photos relating to her more youthful years – the attention she generated as a spectacle with her love of snakes, her many marriages, as well as her entire lifestyle – all demonstrate what, I believe, was the unfulfilled life she chose.

Gertrude died at the age of 89, several years after her husband William's death. She spent her final years in a nursing home. The county in which she resided asked each of her four children for monetary help when her funds were depleted. All four declined. The oldest son, Merton, oversaw her affairs until her death in 1976. After her death, he was asked about the loss of his mother. He answered, "I lost her when I was a child."

My mother was immensely affected by her mother's rejection and lifestyle. She tried to forgive her only to be hurt repeatedly. She did find solace as well as a bit of humor in my declaration: could she imagine what kind of person she would have become if Gertrude would have raised her?!

One of the effects of Gertrude's behavior and leaving her children was that Merton, Earl, and Jeanette all developed a distrust of women. Their youngest brother George didn't seem to be as affected or he didn't remember as much because of his young age.

My cousins (Gertrude's grandchildren), perplexed with calling her "Grandma Matthews" or "Grandma Bell," finally refer to her as "Gertrude, the one who ran off with the choir director, joined the circus, and always wrote using green ink."

I inquired on the name Gertrude in the book *Girls' Christian Names* by Helena Swan. Helena reports it is a German name having to do with strife and battle. From Gar, "Ger"- a spear, we have war, and "trude" means maiden, making the combination, "spear maiden." Our family has not passed on the name Gertrude.

# THE IMPACT OF TRAGEDY

## EVERYTHING I'VE EVER LOVED IS TAKEN AWAY FROM ME

Harvey Wentland passed away on December 30, 1976, at the age of 65. My mother was at work and made her usual mid-morning call to check on him. After several attempts without an answer, she called the ambulance to their home. Minutes later, she arrived. Having found him dead on the sofa, the paramedics told my mother that he had a smile on his face. My belief is that he was reunited with his twins who died 21 years previously.

Shortly after my dad's death, my mother began dating Cliff who had lost his wife only weeks before my dad died. Cliff had a construction company in Berlin and he and his wife knew my parents. The two mourned the losses of their spouses together and later became good friends. He was a nice man and provided many things my mother was never able to experience. They traveled together, enjoyed dining out, danced, and spent time with family. She was happy.

Cliff often boasted that he could dial my mother's phone number in the dark – they had rotary dials at that time. One night, he called her saying, "Jeanette, I'm sick. Get an ambulance." She said she would be right out there. On her way, she stopped at the police department. My mother arrived behind the ambulance to find Cliff dead. She notified his children.

My brother Jack died of a fatal head injury on December 3, 1978, at the age of 39. After feeding his animals in the basement where he housed them for the winter, it was determined that ice on the bottom of his shoes caused him to slip on the painted steps and he hit his head on his basement floor. He had a successful veterinary practice in Kenosha, Wisconsin. Jack was survived by his wife Vickey and her three children whom he had adopted. My mother remarked as we prepared to attend his funeral, "Everything I've ever loved is taken away from me."

My mother found two other acquaintances dead and notified their families. She found a neighbor man dead in his home after he had spent the morning shoveling snow. On her way to work that morning she spoke to him ending the conversation saying he should "take it easy" shoveling. When she arrived home later that day and saw no lights on in his home, she found him dead. Another time, she was checking on a neighbor who had not raised her shade for the day, her signal that she was up and about. When my mom knocked at her door, she heard a faint "come in" and found the lady in a chair gasping for breath. My mother was asked to notify the family, who called the ambulance. The neighbor lady died at the hospital later that evening.

Jeanette made several housing moves after Harvey's death and was situated in an apartment complex on the west side of Berlin. A tornado hit the building where she lived tearing off the roof above her unit. The roof landed on her car causing considerable damage to the vehicle and trauma to my mother. She was fearful of storms and bad weather throughout her life, and this exacerbated her fear. After she spent a night in a shelter, we were allowed to enter the city, pick her up, and take her to our house. She lived at our home for two months until her apartment was ready for occupancy.

My husband Butch and I saw noticeable personality changes beginning to take place. She frequently spoke of tornadoes and storms. Her interests slowly declined and her eating habits changed. Smoking cigarettes seemed to be her foremost activity. When the confusion of days, nights, and dates became apparent, we found an assisted living facility for her in Oshkosh.

My mother Jeanette celebrating her 70th birthday

Jeanette handled the move very well and remarked that she knew she needed assistance in her daily routine. I was pleased to know she was in good hands and to hear her say she "felt like a queen" because she no longer had to cook meals. For two months, she and I were able to spend quality time together every day.

My mother made a practice of walking me to my car after each visit. We always gave each other a hug before I left. One of the last times, we were walking to my car and began talking about the loss of the twins. As we gave each other a hug, we tearfully asked each other simultaneously, "What did we ever do?" This was a question without an answer.

On September 29, 1995, my mother fell and broke her hip. After surgery, she was placed in a nursing home for rehabilitation. She never regained the ability to walk without assistance. Her fight for life and her mental capabilities quickly declined. Her speech became limited to only a few words of a thought. I read some of the stories to her that I had written about our family growing up in California. They were happy stories about us going to the beach, Daddy fishing, and our dog Brownie. She said she "didn't remember any of that stuff anymore." Her life continued with confusion, sadness, withdrawal, and dementia.

While I was pushing her in her wheelchair one day, she asked "Where are they living?" followed by "Are they OK?" I assured her by answering, "I know everyone is fine. We don't need to worry." Another time, with tears in her eyes, she remarked, "They were gone for a long time." She added, "I wish it didn't happen" and "I'm afraid." It was heartbreaking for me to hear her questions and statements.

With her limited mental capacity and after three days of attempts, she was finally able to say the three words "I love you." As we embraced, I was able to say the same three words to her. It was helpful to both of us to express those feelings.

Jeanette Wentland passed away on January 9, 2000, with her family by her side. As my husband and I, our daughters Kim and Kristin (who was pregnant with Jeanette's first great-grandchild) sat beside her holding her hand, she quietly slipped away. I watched the worried tension on her face fade away and be replaced with peace as she went on her way to reunite with her loving husband and children. She was a courageous lady.

*Jo Ann Wentland Koch*

## THE AFTERMATH

The effects of the polio tragedy in my family have been felt ever since it occurred in 1955. My brother Jack always felt that the polio virus was the cause of my developing diabetes. Medical professionals have stated that a virus, stress, or shock can weaken a person's resistance allowing other diseases to follow. In this case, it is believed, my immune system couldn't fight the disease known as diabetes. Diabetes is a condition in which the body is unable to convert sugar from food into energy. Thankfully, insulin was discovered in 1922 and produced on a large scale in 1926.

There are two types of diabetes. Type I, also known as "Juvenile," is usually diagnosed in younger years up into 20-year-olds (and even older). Type I Diabetes is the lack of production of insulin and is treated with insulin injections. Type II, also known as "adult onset," can be treated, often simply by losing weight, exercising, watching diet, or oral medication. Insulin is an option. Type II is resistant to responding to a normal supply of insulin.

At the tender age of 16, three-and-a-half years after the polio event, I was diagnosed as a diabetic. I was an active junior in Berlin High School, just elected for the Junior Prom Court, and busy in many of the school activities. Plans were being made to have our senior class pictures taken and to decide on a college.

On prom night in May, parents were invited to attend the dance when the court was introduced. One of the mothers who hadn't seen me in several weeks noted that I did not look well when I was introduced. She remarked to a nearby friend that I certainly looked "sickly." The following week I was admitted to the Berlin Hospital and thankful I didn't miss the important prom.

In May 1959, I began losing weight, falling asleep in my school classes, drinking excessive amounts of water, and feeling fatigued. Due to frequently having to urinate, I wouldn't dare sneeze or cough. I told my parents that I knew something was wrong and was finally taken to our family doctor. After extensive testing, my diagnosis was Type I Diabetes. I remember thinking it was an "old person's" disease. My step-grandmother had it; however, no diabetes was in my genetic family.

In examining my diagnosis, I resolved "at least it wouldn't be like polio and take my life." My early treatment was one daily injection of long-lasting insulin with several daily urine tests and monthly blood draws. The blood was sent to Madison for evaluation with results arriving one week later. This test was important for adjusting my medication. I learned the importance of diet and exercise, and I struggled to keep urine tests free of sugar. I became active once again and was grateful to know diabetes would allow me to live a long, normal life. I recorded in my diary, "it feels so good to feel good again"; although I felt at that time, if I lived to the age of 25, I would have lived a long life. That thought changed when I actually became 25 years old. At that time, I was married and had a baby. Life was just beginning.

Several weeks after my diagnosis, a young 10-year-old girl, who lived in my neighborhood, was diagnosed with Type I Diabetes. She died. I then became aware that diabetes could kill and that life is fragile. I felt sorry about the young girl's death and the heartache her family was experiencing. As I began learning more about my disease, I realized the seriousness of staying in control and of the possible ugly consequences if I didn't follow the program. I knew that my choices to live a healthy life were up to *me*. I discovered it was necessary for me to ignore the criticism from non-diabetic peers.

My diet had to be greatly modified for a 16-year-old growing girl. My first instructions stressed avoiding sugar. That statement wasn't entirely correct as most foods naturally turn to sugar. In my diet education classes, I learned foods to avoid and healthy foods to include. My working mother – bless her heart – in following my "new diet," fried me an egg with bacon including toast and butter every morning before I went to school. Liver was good – full of iron. The rule was to eat meals on time and to eat the same amount of calories per meal each day to keep urine readings under control. Within the past 53 years, the diabetic diet has made a dramatic change. Calories are no longer counted. Eggs, bacon, butter, and meats are to be limited, and organ meats are no longer healthy. The number of carbohydrates is counted and small servings of cookies and cakes are acceptable. The rule now is "everything in moderation." It is important to be honest with ourselves as diabetes is said to be "the sneaky disease" as well as "the silent killer."

My life was back to normal and I was pleased that exercise was important as I always was an active girl. A walk to Good's Drug Store after school was often a social time for my friends and me. We would sit on the high stools at the soda fountain and order a cherry coke, lime phosphate, or a dish of ice cream before going home. One day, the store proprietors took me aside and gave me the option of buying a pint of "diabetic ice cream" that I could have served to me when I was with friends. My ice cream was in a cooler along with the regular ice cream in an inconspicuous place that only I knew. Again, the people of Berlin were thoughtful and supportive of my family, and I thanked them for their support and kindness.

After graduation from high school, I attended Central State College in Stevens Point, Wisconsin, and lived on the first floor of a dormitory. The first floor housed students who had health needs. Two doors down the hall lived a beautiful girl who was a polio victim in the 1950s. She wore braces on both legs and needed to use wooden crutches. I was apprehensive about befriending her as she reminded me too much of my sister Jeanie. There also was a girl, Donna, who had a congenital birth defect and needed aluminum forearm crutches. I was friends with her and amazed at her mobility and active life. The dormitory housemother, who was a nurse, refrigerated my insulin in her living quarters. Every morning she would set it out by her door for me to draw my dosage for the day.

Keeping insulin refrigerated often created problems. When traveling, I would wrap the insulin bottle to keep it cool. In my purse, I carried a glass syringe in an empty Alka-Seltzer bottle filled with alcohol. The tricky part was keeping my purse upright at all times as the bottle had a tendency to leak. I had two glass syringes and two stainless steel needles sharpened as needed by the pharmacist or my father. When they began hooking on the cotton balls at the bottom of my Alka-Seltzer bottle, I knew it was time to have them sharpened. In the early 1960s this was the novel and appreciated way of staying healthy.

The discovery of insulin in the 1920s was a big step in treating the disease; before that, diabetics died. The initial sources of insulin were from cows, horses, pigs, and fish. By the mid-1970s insulin purity improved and was advanced to human insulin. When I was in college, I had an electric sterilizer where I would sterilize the syringe and needle every morning for five minutes. The sterilizer was a new item that made my life a tad easier.

Blood testing machines became available in the 1970s, allowing better control of blood sugar. Until that time, patients had to test their urine. The 1980s brought disposable syringes and several types of automatic injectors making injections easier at alternate sites. Arm, leg, butt, stomach – my husband was my personal automatic injector.

Adults with Type II Diabetes often are treated with an oral medication. Their pancreas can supply a small amount of insulin, but not enough to handle what is needed for their body. Oftentimes a new diet and loss of several pounds can eliminate the need for medication. Newer supplies and treatments became more sophisticated as years passed. A handy pen contains an insulin vial, syringe, and needle all in one, making eating out and traveling more convenient and refrigeration unnecessary. Having various options of administering insulin are helpful in living a more normal life.

Insulin pump therapy was introduced in the 1980s and is still popular in controlling blood sugar readings. The pump must be worn 24 hours a day as it is programmed to deliver insulin at each individual's need. Mine is a computerized device about the size of a cell phone that is connected to my abdomen by means of an introducer needle surrounded by a Teflon cannula. After inserting the needle and taping it in place, it is withdrawn leaving only the cannula. The site needs to be changed every three days. I have been using a pump for over 15 years and find it keeps me in better control and is the most convenient of any of my previous therapy treatments. A non-diabetic person's pancreas releases insulin as needed throughout a 24-hour period; my insulin pump releases insulin as I need it.

Insulin in a nasal spray is a new medication getting ready to hit the market. New technology is introducing products rapidly with the ultimate goal of producing an artificial pancreas. I am thankful that diabetes control for the young will continue to become easier and healthier allowing them to avoid nasty complications and live normal and productive lives.

The student population of Berlin High School in the early 60s was slightly more than 500. Only three of us were diabetic. The number has increased drastically over the years as children became inactive, weren't encouraged to exercise or eat healthy. It was the beginning of fast-food establishments and popular pizza parlors. Eating meals at home with the family became less routine. This began an epidemic of children developing Type II Diabetes, borderline diabetes, or insulin-dependent diabetes while in middle and high school.

When I was diagnosed with diabetes, my mother was grateful that I didn't have the "awful thing that Chuckie had." Chuckie was my husband Butch's brother who died of leukemia at the age of seven, six months after my diagnosis. His funeral was the first funeral I had been to since my siblings' funerals. I found it horrifying viewing the sweet little child who wanted to be a fireman when he grew up.

I have been a diabetic for 53 years and don't feel I've missed anything life has to offer because of my disease. The best blessings I have experienced are the births of our two healthy daughters. During pregnancy, diabetic women are known to miscarry, or deliver a stillborn or premature baby. I didn't experience complications that were detrimental to our two girls or myself. I feel I have lived a healthier and safer life because I worked hard to follow the program.

## COMPLICATIONS DO OCCUR

"She is in shape . . . . . attends aerobic classes . . . . . a diabetic for 30 years . . . . never has smoked. Monday? We'll make arrangements." I heard half of the telephone conversation taking place outside the door of room 243 in the Intensive Care Unit on the second floor at Mercy Medical Center in Oshkosh. Dr. Al-Nouri returned to my room. With his Syrian accent, he announced to my husband and me that he had just spoken with the "best heart surgeon in the state" and my surgery was scheduled for Monday, January 29, 1990, at St. Luke's Medical Center in Milwaukee. Dr. Al-Nouri had spoken to one of the only two heart surgeons that he would recommend for my case "if they would take" me.

Two days before this conversation, I was an active wife and mother. Caring for my 18-month-old nephew, Justin, was my weekday job along with my commitment to exercising, volunteering, and working with my husband in his business. Keeping my diabetes under control was a daily task and something that I never found to be difficult. I was a healthy 47-year-old . . . so I thought. My husband Butch and I, along with three other couples, had just spent the weekend cross-country skiing in northern Wisconsin.

It didn't matter that I had invited two friends for lunch that day. Or that our two daughters had just left for a semester of college in England.

Or that Butch and I were planning to attend a Super Bowl party the next week. Our schedule came to a sudden halt. We had something more important that needed our undivided attention. Undivided it was when Butch announced, "We are in this together."

We called our daughters, Kim and Kristin. They asked if they should return home for which we immediately replied, "No." We assured them they would be kept informed through "Ma Bell." We often talked by telephone which was assurance to all of us that we were together in this trial.

I enjoyed the many visitors who stopped at the hospital to wish me well, and I was comforted with Butch next to me, his arm gently around my shoulder.

Soon, terror struck! Death was a reality. Was God going to take me? Did He realize what He was doing? I tried to look into the small mirror kept in the drawer next to my hospital bed. I could only glimpse, as what I saw looking back at me was a face full of fear and eyes that no longer sparkled. I truly was afraid to face the next step.

The ambulance ride to St. Luke's Medical Center was delayed one day due to a typical January snowstorm. I was happy to spend one more day with the caring staff at Mercy. They showed compassion along with my family doctor, Dr. Weston, who wished me well with the promise he would be praying for me.

Finally, it was Monday, and I was prepared for surgery. Friends and relatives from all over the U.S. and Europe had contacted me and were offering prayers. My pastor and his wife visited me. It was time for the inevitable. Surgery was completed within three-and-a-half hours. Dr. Tector's team kept Butch informed as it progressed. Dr. Al-Nouri's assessment of "considerable artery damage" was verified by the seven by-passes I received that day.

The following Sunday I returned home. My healing was achieved by patience, rest, and rehabilitation. Our daughters returned from a wonderful five-and-a-half months in Europe to a healthy mom and grateful dad. I continued exercising, volunteering, and working with my husband. My luncheons, skiing trips, and Super Bowl parties were enjoyed again along with the green grass, flowers, light of each new day, and life.

# MY CHRISTIAN FAITH

Within a six-day period, my sister and brother died from polio and my brother John was rushed to the same hospital with a diagnosis of polio. My mother said to me, "The doctors told me they had done all they could and John was now in the hands of God." The words "in the hands of God" became etched permanently in my 12-year-old mind. That inspiring comment, especially from a medical doctor, was the genesis of my spiritual belief.

Two months later, my brother John returned home from the overwhelmed polio ward. At this time, I became firm in my belief that Jesus loved me and answered my prayers to save my brother; He would always be with me. Prayer filled the void and remains with me today. It fills my heart and mind with compassion for others.

I was diagnosed with insulin-dependent diabetes when I was 16 years old. I never asked "why me?" but more "why not me?" My first thoughts were that I can manage this disease and it doesn't need to be fatal. I also thought my experience would allow me to help others. My prayers still include gratitude for helping me accept this ailment, asking God for strength to eat healthy and take care of myself.

At the age of 47, I was diagnosed with heart disease and survived a seven-bypass heart surgery. I was fearful of the disease as well as the surgery. My prayerful husband was a significant support, staying by my side and encouraging my recovery. Prayer was important at this frightening and stressful time. Friends and relatives all over the United States as well as our two daughters, studying in England for a semester, prayed on my behalf. I was thankful to have their prayerful support for recovery and convalescing. It has been 23 years since the surgery, and every day I am grateful for my health and my active lifestyle.

I believe that everyone is born with a purpose and a gift. I feel my gift is prayer as well as compassion for others. Maybe those harsh words, "If you cry, you are selfish," I heard at the age of 12 were a blessing that signified my mission in life. My gift is effortless and one I can perform at any time anywhere. Prayer for me does not need a formal setting nor be spoken out loud. My prayers come from my heart and mind and are offered while walking behind a lawn mower, driving a car, or preparing a meal. They are not formal as heard from the mouth of a minister. They are simply spoken in my own humble words. I believe prayer has helped me to be a better person.

Jo and Butch, Alaska – 2001

## THE HORRIFIC LOSS OF CHILDREN

My mother and I visited the cemetery together on the anniversary dates of the twins' birthdays and deaths. When our first daughter, Kim, was nine months old and we were visiting the graves, I held my baby tightly as I asked my mother, "How did you ever stand losing your children?" There was no answer.

Twins, Jeanie and Georgie, at their second birthdays - June 13, 1943

After experiencing the loss of children, people going through the same tragedy would sometimes turn to my mother for advice. She was always supportive but didn't have any sage guidance to offer as she often wept with them. Over the years, she was asked to speak to groups on experiencing the loss of children. I never attended any of her talks but knew it was always difficult for her to recall the devastation her family endured.

Years after Jeanie's and Georgie's deaths, my mother shared a recurring dream with me. She dreamed she was calling the twins for dinner. They answered her from outside, around the corner of the house. When they were about to come around the corner, my mother would abruptly awaken, never seeing them.

I have not seen my siblings together in a dream. Although as I write this story, I dreamed a repeat of the last time Georgie and I played together, the night of Jeanie's funeral. He and I were pinching each other. In the dream I could feel how warm his skin was because he was feverish, and I remember noticing the freckles on his face. I enjoyed having that experience.

A passage I found in the NIV Bible that I feel defines my mother and me is: 2 Corinthians 1: verses 3, 4, and 5: Praise be to the God and Father of our Lord Jesus Christ, the Father of compassion and the God of all comfort; who comforts us in all our troubles, so that we can comfort those in any trouble with the comfort we ourselves have received from

God. For just as the sufferings of Christ flow over into our lives, so also through Christ our comfort overflows.

# UPDATE ON THE STATUS OF POLIO,

# AS OF 6/11/2012

Via email from Kris Tsau, granddaughter of Mr. Carter, the photographer who saved the photos from the fire:

"One of the biggest challenges we face in this country is that the younger generations have no real fear or memory of polio and don't really understand what a threat it can be. This had been made worse by misinformation that incorrectly has linked autism to the use of vaccines.

To answer your questions: There have been no endemic cases of polio in the United States since 1979 (this means the virus that originated here in the United States). There have been rare cases of imported polio virus. This means that someone who had not been immunized caught the virus from someone who came from somewhere else who was infected. The United States and many countries around the world have very high levels of immunization, so this is usually not too big a threat for us, but imported cases of polio from countries where it still exists will continue to pose a risk until polio has been completely eradicated, like small pox.

The good news is that we have never been closer to achieving polio eradication. Only three countries: Afghanistan, Pakistan, and Nigeria, have never stopped transmission of polio. Every other country, including the most populous nations of China and India, and troubled places like Angola and Sudan, have been able to stop transmission. At his point in 2012, there have been only 64 children who have contracted polio this year. That is the lowest number in recorded history.

You can imagine that Nigeria, Pakistan, and Afghanistan are some of the most difficult countries to work in, but there is an unprecedented effort to finish the job in these countries and the neighboring countries that remain at risk.

There is no cure for polio, unfortunately. However, the disease is preventable through vaccination (either the Salk injectable vaccine used in most developed countries or the Sabin, oral vaccine used in most of the rest of the world).

Poor sanitation is certainly a factor in the spread of polio, but the virus cannot be transmitted by other animals. This is one of the scientific reasons that polio was chosen as a disease that the world could work to eradicate."

From the Global Polio Eradication Initiative website, (http:www.polioeradication.org-/Polioandprevention.aspx):

## *Polio and prevention*

Polio is a crippling and potentially fatal infectious disease. There is no cure, but there are safe and effective vaccines. The strategy to eradicate polio is therefore based on preventing infection by immunizing every child until transmission stops and the world is polio-free.

*The disease*

Polio (poliomyelitis) is a highly infectious disease caused by a virus. It invades the nervous system and can cause irreversible paralysis in a matter of hours.

**Who is at risk?**

Polio can strike at any age, but it mainly affects children under five years old.

*Transmission*

Polio is spread through person-to-person contact. When a child is infected with wild poliovirus, the virus enters the body through the mouth and multiplies in the intestine. It is then shed into the environment through the faeces where it can spread rapidly through a community, especially in situations of poor hygiene and sanitation. If a sufficient number of children are fully immunized against polio, the virus is unable to find susceptible children to infect, and dies out.

Young children who are not yet toilet-trained are a ready source of transmission, regardless of their environment. Polio can be spread when food or drink is contaminated by faeces. There is also evidence that flies can passively transfer poliovirus from faeces to food.

Most people infected with the poliovirus have no signs of illness and are never aware they have been infected. These symptomless people carry the virus in their intestines and can "silently" spread the infection to thousands of others before the first case of polio paralysis emerges. For this reason, WHO considers a single confirmed case of polio paralysis to be evidence of an epidemic – particularly in countries where very few cases occur.

*Symptoms*

Most infected people (90%) have no symptoms or very mild symptoms and usually go unrecognized. In others, initial symptoms include fever, fatigue, headache, vomiting, stiffness in the neck and pain in the limbs.

**Acute flaccid paralysis (AFP)**

One in 200 infections leads to irreversible paralysis, usually in the legs. This is caused by the virus entering the blood stream and invading the central nervous system. As it multiplies, the virus destroys the nerve cells that activate muscles. The affected muscles are no longer functional and the limb becomes floppy and lifeless – a condition known as acute flaccid paralysis (AFP).

All cases of acute flaccid paralysis (AFP) among children under fifteen years of age are reported and tested for poliovirus within 48 hours of onset.

*Bulbar polio*

More extensive paralysis, involving the trunk and muscles of the thorax and abdomen, can result in quadriplegia. In the most severe cases (bulbar polio), poliovirus attacks the nerve cells of the brain stem, reducing breathing capacity and causing difficulty in swallowing and speaking. Among those paralyzed, 5% to 10% die when their breathing muscles become immobilized.

In the 1940s and 1950s, people with bulbar polio were immobilized inside "iron lungs" – huge metal cylinders that operated like a pair of bellows to regulate their breathing and keep them alive. Today, the iron lung has largely been replaced by the positive pressure ventilator, but it is still in use in some countries.

185

**Post-polio syndrome**

Around 40% of people who survive paralytic polio may develop additional symptoms 15–40 years after the original illness. These symptoms – called post-polio syndrome – include new progressive muscle weakness, severe fatigue and pain in the muscles and joints.

*Risk factors for paralysis*

No one knows why only a small percentage of infections lead to paralysis. Several key risk factors have been identified as increasing the likelihood of paralysis in a person infected with polio. These include:

- immune deficiency
- pregnancy
- removal of the tonsils (tonsillectomy)
- intramuscular injections, e.g. medications
- strenuous exercise
- injury.

*Treatment and prevention*

There is no cure for polio, only treatment to alleviate the symptoms. Heat and physical therapy is used to stimulate the muscles and antispasmodic drugs are given to relax the muscles. While this can improve mobility, it cannot reverse permanent polio paralysis. Polio can be prevented through immunization. Polio vaccine, given multiple times, almost always protects a child for life.

# Jo and Butch's Family

Top, left to right: Jo and Butch Koch
Center adults, left to right: Kristin & Norman Bock, Kirk & Kim Hartman
Children on laps, left to right: Julia, Isaac, & Charlie Bock
Photo courtesy of Limelite Photography Studio, Oshkosh, WI

Left to right: Jo, daughters Kim and Kristin, and Butch
Spring 2012